REALM OF THE FOX

INDIAN INTELLIGENCE AND THE SPECTRE OF THE DARK ENEMY

C.P. THOMAS

Notion Press

No.8, 3rd Cross Street,
CIT Colony, Mylapore,
Chennai, Tamil Nadu – 600004

First Published by Notion Press 2020
Copyright © C.P. Thomas 2020
All Rights Reserved.

ISBN 978-1-64850-902-5

ABOUT THE AUTHOR

The author originally hails from Kerala. After completing his MA in Economics, he worked briefly as a lecturer in industrial economics before joining the Intelligence Bureau (IB) in 1970. He served the Bureau for over 38 years in various capacities and was posted at more than 14 locations across the length and breadth of the country before his superannuation in 2008 as Assistant Director, IB.

After demitting from the IB, he went on to pursue a PhD in Administration and Policing. By virtue of his long service in the IB, particularly in its various operational matters, the author was able to understand the ins and outs of the intelligence system not only in India but also in some of the most important countries in the world.

This book is dedicated to my wife and children, and all my colleagues in the department for their support, encouragement and assistance in all the difficulties and challenges faced during the service.

My special thanks are due to Shri Sudhir Kumar, IPS, who retired from IB as Special Director and then Vigilance Commissioner, Government of India, for kindly writing the foreword for this book. He was one of the most outstanding officers, the epitome of knowledge, a perfect gentleman and, above all, a fine human being while dealing with subordinates.

– C.P. Thomas

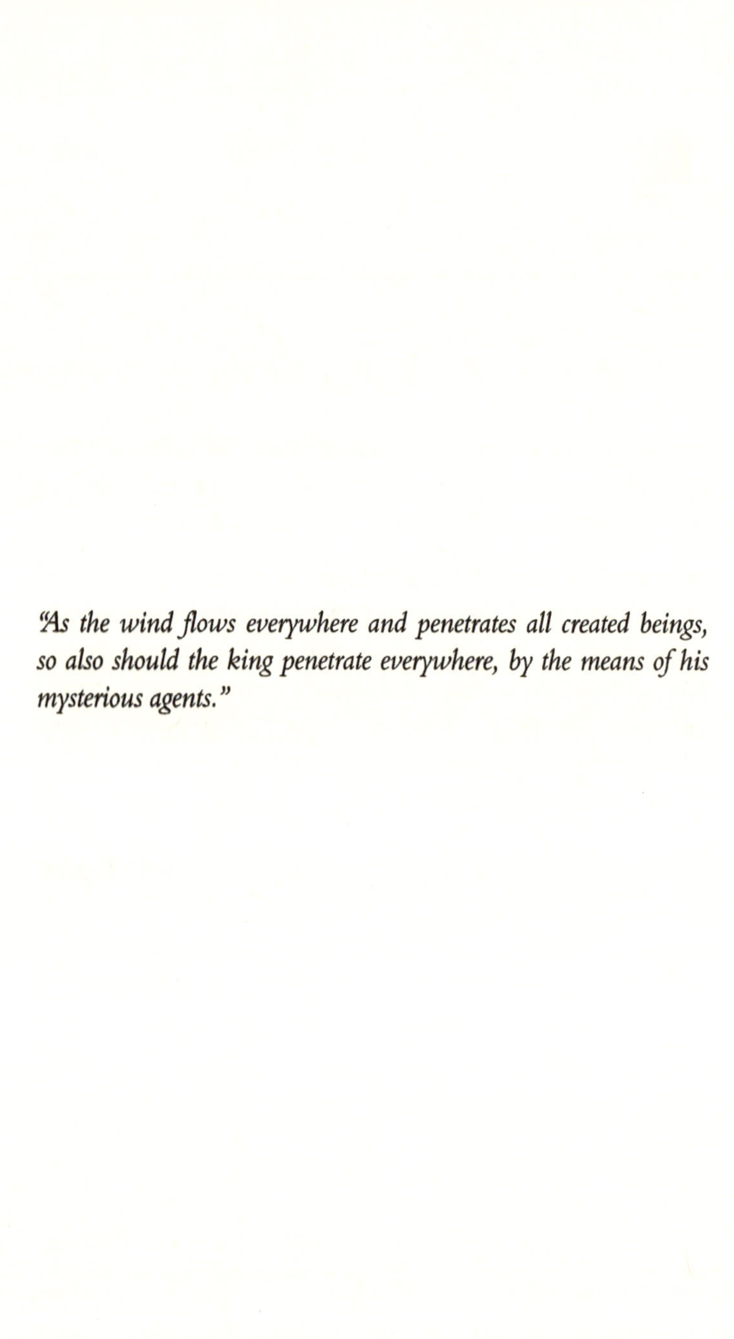

"As the wind flows everywhere and penetrates all created beings, so also should the king penetrate everywhere, by the means of his mysterious agents."

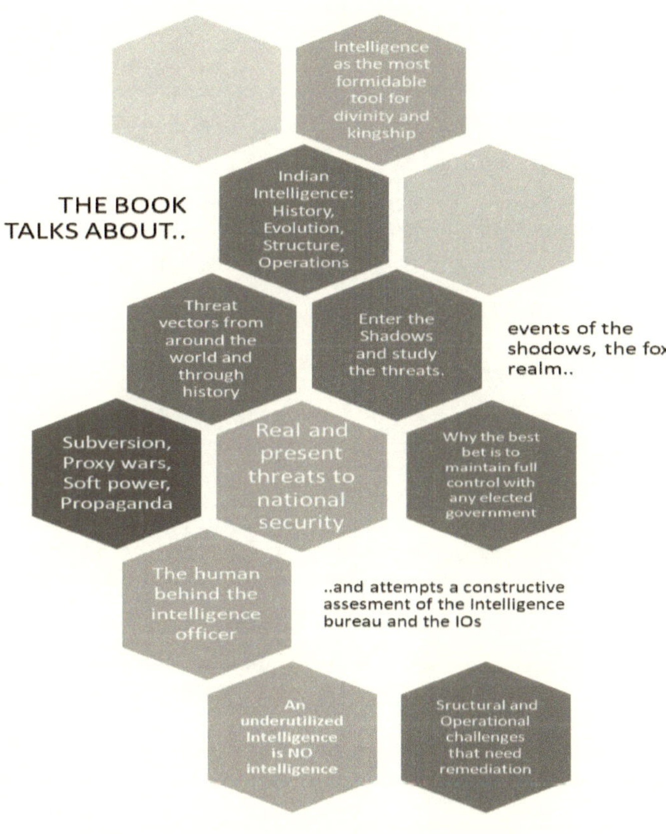

THE BOOK TALKS ABOUT..

Intelligence as the most formidable tool for divinity and kingship

Indian Intelligence: History, Evolution, Structure, Operations

Threat vectors from around the world and through history

Enter the Shadows and study the threats.

events of the shodows, the fox realm..

Subversion, Proxy wars, Soft power, Propaganda

Real and present threats to national security

Why the best bet is to maintain full control with any elected government

The human behind the intelligence officer

..and attempts a constructive assesment of the Intelligence bureau and the IOs

An underutilized Intelligence is NO intelligence

Sructural and Operational challenges that need remediation

CONTENTS

Preface   *11*

Foreword   *15*

Intelligence Gathering: Origin and Quintessence

1. Omniscience and Espionage   21

2. Intelligence Gathering: The Science of It   27

Intelligence Bureau: Structure and Operations

3. Intelligence Bureau: Evolution and Constitution   41

4. Operational Matters   50

National Security Threats and Intelligence Operations: The Shadow Games

5. Trans-Border Intelligence   57

6. Political Parties   64

7. Religious Fundamentalism   73

8. Narco-Terrorism   90

Contents

9. Biological Sabotage: The Chinese
Threat and Bioterrorism 95

10. Naxalism: Armed Rebellion Against the
Government and Democracy 113

11. Rebellion Against Government and Democracy:
The Looming Threat of the Non-State Actors 123

12. Cyberspace 133

13. Money Laundering, Human/Drug Trafficking 149

14. Non-Governmental Organisations 166

Master of Intelligence.
Using Our Nation's Intelligence Faculties

15. Real and Present Dangers to the
Establishment and the Nation 177

16. Subversion and the Overthrow
of the Establishment 182

17. Threat To The Head Of State 194

The Force on the Ground Integrity, Discipline and
Other People Challenges of the IOs and the Police

18. Corruption and Nepotism 223

19. Discipline in Police and
Intelligence Organisations 234

20. Heroes are human too 241

21. Suggestions and Comments 250

22. In Conclusion 253

PREFACE

outfox

verb

(Informal) *To defeat (someone) by being more clever or cunning than them.*

Intelligence officers are a set of people who are unknown, unassuming and engaged in undercover jobs. Even within the organisation, one should know only what he or she is supposed to know, and nothing more. Any eagerness to know what is not required as per the intelligence norms is considered a failure on the part of the officer and against the principle of restrictive security followed by intelligence agencies throughout the world as a basic tenet of intelligence work.

The public comes to know of an intelligence operation only when there is a failure. Though 99 times out of a hundred intelligence inputs might have saved lives and property worth crores, a single failure tarnishes the image of the intelligence officers—this happened recently after the brutal killing of nearly 40 CRPF jawans on the Jammu–

Srinagar highway in an ISI-sponsored suicide attack. What is not widely known is that the Intelligence Bureau (IB) prevented five major attacks planned by Islamic terrorists during the 2019 Republic Day celebrations. There have been hundreds of such incidents, ever since the day of India's Independence, in which the IB, the topmost internal security organisation of the country, has been successful in preventing heinous crimes and national loss.

An intelligence officer's spirit of patriotism and dedication to duty leads him or her to discharge his or her duties to the best of his or her ability and to the utmost satisfaction of the government. Undoubtedly, intelligence work is very difficult and complicated. Only skilled personnel can undertake this work. Intelligence officers are the eyes and ears of the government and the nation. They keep their eyes and ears open—but their mouths shut. There are lacunae and constraints in the work, but a successful Intelligence Officer (IO) depends on his or her ability and efficiency, dedication and ambition to achieve the goal. Unlike other government jobs, including policing, the work of an IO is seldom seen by the general public. The IO lives and dies in the shadows. His battlefield confines to the realms of the darkness against invisible enemy vectors.

The happenings in the shadows, the battles won there on a daily basis, and the assaults the nation thus thwarts remain unseen and unknown to the mainstream media and the general populace.

The threats that the nation faces are many. The enemy is sometimes invisible and nameless, a mere phantom. We live in an era in which continuous threat evaluation is pivotal. A lot needs to be learnt from what is happening elsewhere in the world.

How hostile nations have used subversion and other proxy war tactics against a target nation, how they have sabotaged an elected government, causing its overthrow, how armed rebel groups have succeeded in winning over local allegiances and even international recognition. There are examples from around the world and throughout history. Anyone who thinks that these are problems local to a particular region and cannot happen in our country is misinformed and myopic.

Back in the eighties, no one thought that the CIA model of using the mujahedeen as a proxy weapon could ever be replicated in Kashmir. No one would imagine that computer hackers could bring down critical installations, paralysing a nation.

It is a never-ending game of who outfoxes the other, and the intelligence officer is at the forefront of our nation's defence.

All possible precautions have been taken to keep secret the nature of IB and its operational functions that are not in the public domain. There could be some repetitions or points with synonymous meaning in our chapters. It is bound to happen as all materials on intelligence are interconnected and correlated.

FOREWORD

What has been the single most potent weapon of warfare in history? What has been the one thing that separated the offensive strategies of the victor, who took it all, and the vanquished, who burned in hellfire?

Whether it is the 'Game of Thrones' that went on through millennia between kingdoms or the proxy wars being fought out in the shadows among the nations today, Information and Intelligence have been the key to success. In contemporary times, where world organisations exist to preserve the current world order and try to rein in the rogue nations, an outright war may not be a viable option.

But discreet or covert methods, duly backed by sound intelligence, provide a pragmatic cost-effective alternative. Modern-day warfare resembles moves on a chessboard, and what has become most important today, is anticipating the opponent's next move. Mind games have turned into a major force multiplier for the ever-sharpening arms race.

C.P. Thomas, the author of this book, has been a battle-hardened Intelligence Officer (IO), who has had long years of varied experience in sensitive areas of national security. He has personally gone through the trials and tribulations and experienced the successes and failures first-hand as the foot soldier of India's premier security agency, the Intelligence Bureau (IB).

This book, which benefits from the author's life experiences, is a commendable documentation of various researches into areas such as the threats to national security, the IB's track record of coping with the challenges it faces and the imperatives for the future.

The tone of the book is generally analytical, but it is also critical where the weaknesses and shortcomings, individual or institutional, need to be addressed. As one reads through the book, one cannot help admiring the effort that has gone into its making, while keeping the focus on the core issues and objectives pertaining to the nation's security. It is gratifying that the author has deftly handled sensitive issues to inform the reader without compromising the basic tenets of organisational and professional secrecy.

The book is a systematic and painstaking compilation of a lot of information available in the public domain, but rekindles the memory of incidents, both global events as well as national, going as far back as the nineteen fifties with an analytical and introspective vigour.

It delves into national security and organisational matters, while presenting the IO, the spy, as a human with natural ambitions, emotions, ego, yearnings and professional jealousies. It emphasises that the nation's spies and men of forces in real life and blood are so drastically different from the celluloid Bollywood heroes; the selfless and self-effacing operatives who don't seek adulation, and are people with families and personal lives, as gullible and fallible as anyone. It discusses the conflicts at work as well as the fault lines and gaps in the system that require systemic attention.

More importantly, the book seeks introspection on the vital question of whether we have equipped our agencies and use them well enough to defend against the covert assaults of various shadowy enemies.

It provides suggestions and makes a case for why an adequately equipped and empowered professional intelligence agency is an absolute must for India in these times of internal strife and externally engineered subversions and proxy wars.

There is a hidden enemy design behind most of the disruptive and destructive acts that happen around to impede the country's forward march.

Towards the end, the author attempts to drive home the point on who should wield absolute power on the nation's intelligence faculties and why.

I personally view this book as a laudable initiative to educate, inform, and generate awareness and discussion on a subject that is extremely vital for national consciousness but has remained too shrouded in secrecy.

Sudhir Kumar, IPS (Retd)

Ex- Special Director, IB

Ex-Vigilance Commissioner, Central Vigilance Commission of India.

Ex-Secretary (Security), Govt, of India.

Intelligence Gathering: Origin and Quintessence

ONE

OMNISCIENCE AND ESPIONAGE

—)•(—

Divinity and kingship's quest to become the 'All-knowing'

Espionage and counterespionage are difficult and only a trained and skilful person can undertake them. It requires courage, total dedication and determination to achieve the required result. As a matter of fact, surveillance or spying has been practised ever since the human race has existed.

In the Abrahamic story of creation, we find that, from the day they were created and allowed to live in the Garden of Eden, the first man and woman were under constant surveillance, not only by God but also by Satan.

The basic principles in spying are to be aware, to gather information and lie in wait and to act only at the appropriate time and place. Satan, who was watching both Adam and Eve, was waiting for a chance to win Eve over, as his study of her showed that she was more breakable, with more anxiety and ambition than Adam.

And so, Satan waited and waited, watching them closely all the while. Finally, when the appropriate time came, Satan succeeded in winning Eve's confidence, convincing her to eat the forbidden fruit. This is exactly what the spy must do. He or she must patiently wait for the suitable time to execute a plan. This one small stroke of manipulative brilliance changed the course of the relationship between man and the divine for all eternity.

'Sin' came into the world. And with one tiny but perfectly executed act, with a carefully planted seed in the mind of his first victim, Satan established his relevance in the world forever. A real smooth operation, one might say.

In order to achieve any task, it is imperative to have extensive information, otherwise known as 'intelligence'. Collecting this intelligence is the paramount duty of an IO or a spy. Intelligence gathering is an ancient profession that can claim scriptural authority from the earliest literature—the Rg Veda and the Puranas.

An inquiry into acts of espionage by ruling administrations in ancient India set me on weeks of research for data. The *Arthashastra*, the Puranas and the Vedas are replete with examples and guidelines on the art of using espionage and intelligence-gathering as instruments for kings and gods. Be it for public administration for the kings or for awareness of all events on earth, the all-knowingness, sheer omniscience for the celestial.

Varuna has been depicted on multiple occasions as the God of the night sky. Hymns of his glorification call the swarms of stars of the night sky 'Varuna's thousand eyes'. With these starry eyes of his, Varuna would watch over all human conduct, and would judge between good and evil.

The Rg Veda refers to his eyes as *spasa*, which was derived from the root word *spek* or to "see", which later evolved into the word "spy".

'He watched over human beings: When two persons conversed, he was the invisible third'

*Source: Encyclopedia Of Oriental Philosophy and Religion: Hinduism

The Gods, it is said, have deputed their trusted spies amidst the blades of grass on the ground, from where, these spies extend to every spot on the planet and observe every event without flickering once. No creature can even wink without their knowledge.

RV VII,61,3: ...Have in the fields and houses set your warder-, who visit every spot and watch unceasingly.*

But such unwavering surveillance is not just an operational necessity for their jobs as celestial grand juries or as superintendents of all happenings on earth; it is indispensable for their very reign as undisputed monarchs of the land. It is what separates Gods from mortals – 'omniscience'.

RV I, 25, 7-10:*

7. He knows the path of birds that fly through heaven, and, Sovran of the sea,

He knows the ships that are thereon.

8. True to his holy law, he knows the twelve moons with their progeny:

He knows the moon of later birth.

9. He knows the pathway of the wind, the spreading, high, and mighty wind:

He knows the Gods who dwell above.

10. Varuna, true to holy law, sits down among his people; he,

Most wise, sits there to govern all.

He governs all, because He is omniscient.

His spies bestow Him with all-encompassing knowledge. And he attains this state of all-knowing because of his 'spasas'.

Sun Tsu mentions the importance of espionage in '*The Art of War*':

Thus, what enables the wise sovereign and the good general to strike and conquer, and achieve things beyond the reach of ordinary men, is foreknowledge. Whether the object be to crush an army, to storm a city, or to assassinate an individual, it is always necessary to begin by finding out the names of the attendants, the aides-de-camp, and door-keepers and sentries of the general in command. Our spies must be commissioned to ascertain these.★

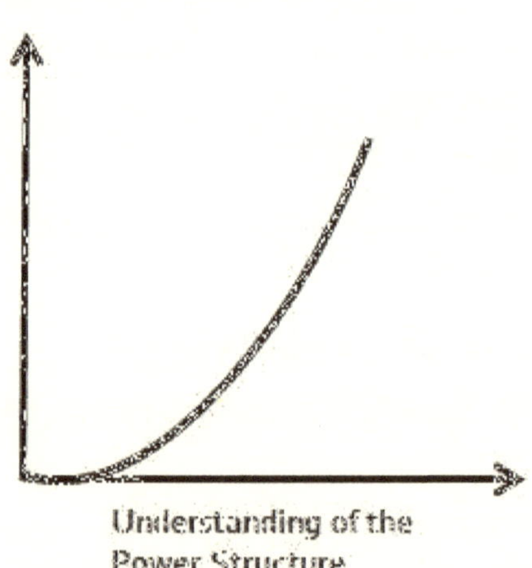

In the *Arthashastra*, Kautilya attempts the systemisation of these scriptural sanctions and other scattered knowledge on the subject and accredits espionage as a crucial apparatus for governance. All of a sudden, espionage was statecraft, needed to ensure the longevity of the King's reign and the general welfare of society. The Puranas, too, have minced no words to deliberate on the art of spying as a necessary adjunct of public administration and have repeatedly advised the ruling classes to use it extensively for human welfare. Bhisma, in the Mahabharata, explains that the ideal means to ensure the success of kingship, is through the institution of espionage. *Mbh, XII, Chap 19, Sl.8,9,11,12★*

His spies should be so employed that they may not know one another.

He should also, O bull of Bharata's race, know the spies of his foes by himself setting spies in shops and places of amusement, and concourses of people, among beggars, in his pleasure gardens and parks, in meetings and conclaves of the learned, in the country, in public places, in places where he holds his own court, and in the houses of the citizens. The king possessed of intelligence may thus ascertain the spies dispatched by his foes.

Enumerating the qualities of spies, Bhisma says he should employ as spies, men looking like idiots or like those that are blind and deaf. Those should all be persons who have been thoroughly examined (in respect of their ability), who are possessed of wisdom, and who are able to endure hunger and thirst. With proper attention, the king should set his spies upon all his counsellors and friends and sons, in his city and the provinces, and in dominions of the chiefs under him

★source: sacred-texts.com

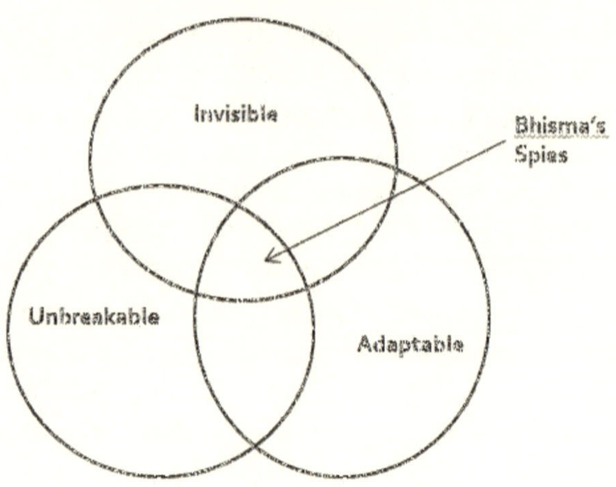

So far, we have seen the relevance of intelligence gathering through the ages.

TWO

INTELLIGENCE GATHERING: THE SCIENCE OF IT

Intelligence analysis aims to reduce the uncertainty in highly ambiguous situations. Many analysts evaluate the high- or low-probability explanations but prefer the middle-of-the-road explanation. A body of specific methods for intelligence analysis is generally referred to as analytic tradecraft. The academic disciplines examining the art and science of intelligence analysis are most routinely referred to as intelligence studies. Pursuit of expertise in analytic tradecraft is the central component of the intelligence plan. While a good analyst must be able to consider, thoughtfully, alternative viewpoints, an analyst must also be willing to stand by his or her position. This is especially important in specialised areas when the analyst may be the only one that reads every field report and every technical observation.

Intelligence analysts are expected to give policymakers the most effective information product, particularly in the following areas: opportunities and dangers in the analyst's country, especially unexpected developments that may require a reaction; motives, objectives, strength and vulnerabilities; allies and other actors. Besides, the information should contain direct and indirect sources of the friendly party's leverage on foreign players and issues and tactical alternatives for advancing stated national policy goals. The analyst is also responsible for organizing raw data, interpolating known data, evaluating the value of data and putting it into a working hypothesis.

Information is of various degrees: direct information can help the analysts and their consumers evaluate the likelihood that something is factual and thereby reduce uncertainty. This includes information related to an intelligence issue under scrutiny, the details of which can be considered factual because of the nature of the source, the source's direct access to the information and the concrete and readily available character of the contents.

Indirect information relating to an intelligence issue includes details which may or may not be factual, or for which there is doubt reflecting some combination of the source's questionable reliability, the source's direct access and the complex character of the contents.

Intelligence can be divided into strategic and operational intelligence.

Strategic intelligence provides policy makers with the information needed to make national policies or decisions of long-lasting importance. It enables formulation of the nation's stand on matters national or international and helps protect and further the national interest.

Intelligence collection for the national strategist's consumption often involves integrating discerning and sophisticated information relating to politics, military affairs, economics, social climate, public perceptions, prevalent propagandas and technological developments.

It feeds the disciplines of intelligence studies and security analysis and typically evolves over a long period of time. The intelligence thus gathered can be used by the government to assess its standing in the general political arena of the nation, or the perception of the people regarding its performance. It can be regarding obtaining credible reports on people's reactions to its policies and suggestions on course corrections that might be needed.

Operational intelligence is a continuing tracking of current affairs, mainly pertaining to real and present dangers to national security and to law and order. It is used to determine the current and projected risk of threat elements on an ongoing basis. Operational intelligence helps thwart threats to the operations of the ruling establishment, and to the general welfare of the country. It can also include counterintelligence and counterespionage functions that execute measures to eliminate adversary theft of national secrets and enemy subversions.

The Analysis Cycle

The intelligence analysis cycle is the process through which the decision for assessment is taken, targets are chosen, intelligence is subsequently gathered, dissected, and interpreted, and recommendations are made available to the masters of intelligence, the ruling government. The cycle below depicts the process used by the primary intelligence agencies around the world.

The steps in the intelligence cycle are as follows:

Requirements and Planning: The first step in the cycle involves the administration of the entire espionage effort, from identifying the need for a threat assessment to the final delivery of the gathered information. The process consists of identification and validation of intelligence requirements, translation of the requirements into observables, decisions on a gathering methodology, initiation of intelligence gathering, dissemination of the intelligence back to the government, and continuous monitoring of the collected information for anomalies and red flags.

Collection: The second step, collection, includes both acquiring information and provisioning forward that information. It encompasses the management of various functions, including gathering strategies. Based upon identified intelligence and the desired observables, the gatherers are tasked to initiate collection.

A number of different intelligence disciplines can be used for collection activities, thus creating duplications in collection streams. Such deliberated redundancies compensate for the potential loss or failure of a collection asset. Any possible failure or compromise of a collection asset is compensated for by a duplicate or different asset who has been facilitating the same collection requirement. Using different types of collection systems also allows for availability of secondary data on the matter. Such collection of different types of information helps to confirm or disprove potential assessments.

Collection operations hence thrive on classified, reliable and redundant information streams. These streams work separately but don't compete. In many cases, they synergize. There is usually a great scope for exchanges of detection, geolocation and targeting information among the collection agents. Agents might cross-cue or tip-off each other to further the shared cause. Once collected, information is correlated and forwarded for analysis and interpretation.

Processing: The third step, processing, is the preparation of collected data into a form suitable for the interpretation of intelligence analysts. Processing may include such activities as translation and reduction of intercepted messages into written formats to permit detailed analysis and comparison with other information. Other types of processing include video production, photographic processing, and correlation of information collected by a variety of technical surveillance platforms.

Interpretation: The fourth step, interpretation, is the process of analysing, evaluating and integrating raw data and information into finished, credible intelligence useable for anticipated purposes and applications. The interpretation may be developed from a single source or from all-source collection and methods. To be effective, interpretation must pivot on the requirement and the direction that was originally given by the administration. The output of Interpretation should be accurate and objective, at the same time should be timely completed. The government expects accurate and actionable inputs and at the right time.

As part of the interpretation process, the analyst must pick and choose, and that is not easy. To that end, the interpreter should eliminate information that is redundant, erroneous, or inapplicable to the intelligence requirement.

He should ensure that the interpretation is done primarily on the matter that he was tasked to study but at the same time should judiciously relay any unrelated red flags he comes across so that the administration can decide to commission new collection requirements and trigger the analysis cycle for those.

During analytical phase, it may be determined that additional information is required to deliberate on an intelligence finding. This will prompt additional collection requirements. The final intelligence interpretation must provide the government with an objective understanding of the subject matter. It should draw analytical conclusions supported by available data.

Dissemination: The final step of the intelligence cycle is dissemination. Dissemination is the conveyance of intelligence to the master of intelligence, the ruling establishment, in a usable form. Intelligence can be provided in a wide range of formats, including verbal reports, written reports, imagery products and statistics. Dissemination can be the handing over of analysed data, as well as recommendations to the government on how the data is to be used and how the government should react in the wake of the new information that has been brought to its notice. However, it is fully the prerogative of the government to accept or ignore these recommendations.

The following section examines the various intelligence collection disciplines and considers their use by adversaries against the nation.

HUMINT

HUMINT, or human intelligence, is derived from human sources. HUMINT in general has become synonymous with espionage and clandestine activities, but in many cases, HUMINT collection can also be performed by overt collectors such as diplomats and military attaches. HUMINT has been the oldest method for collecting information about a foreign power. For most nations in the world, it remains the mainstay of their intelligence collection activities. This has been so even as recently as the 1980s, before the information explosion through the internet and other media.

Overt HUMINT can be performed openly and doesn't bother about protection of the identity of the information collector and his sponsor. Overt HUMINT collectors can include diplomatic personnel, members of official delegations, military attaches and de-briefers at refugee centres. They can collect such HUMINT by studying unclassified publications, conference materials, and collated data from interrogation centres for refugees and prisoners of war.

This can be done by the immigration officers by debriefing legal travellers from destination countries that were of interest to the nation's intelligence service. Diplomats and inspectors employed by world organisations and controlled NGOs can also be specially trained to collect overt as well as classified information while availing diplomatic immunity.

Intrusive on-site inspections provide an extremely useful guise under which these diplomats can gain physical access to sensitive installations, especially on territories that otherwise are kept hidden and inaccessible. And what accord these organisations permit to inspect are the treaties that nations sign to be considered partners with world powers and to escape economic sanctions and other hostilities. The apprehension of being tagged a rogue nation forces the signing of treaties related to nuclear proliferation, chemical warfare, arms reductions, etc., all of which pertain to military sensitive locations. Inspections come as a package deal and substantiate technical data collection to validate declarations. In reality, this opens up opportunities for intrusions into sensitive facilities of other nations. Many of these inspection personnel or NGO activists can be in fact undercover intelligence collectors.

Hence a routine validation of a nation's claim of adherence, using voluntarily furnished data and accesses, can become a sort of a double-faced **'sensitive' HUMINT** mission.

Clandestine HUMINT is a whole different animal as it involves working in the shadows and bringing out specific information, without compromising the identity of the sponsor of the intelligence collection. The activity should always reside in the shadows and the exposure of its existence can result in political embarrassment for the sponsoring nation and its secret initiatives; it can expose its insecurities as well bare its secret ambitions. It can thus sabotage any other mission-critical intelligence operations run by the country.

These are primarily run by the experts, whom we call spies, recruited and trained agents of the nation's intelligence faculties. These can even be converted spies or locals who willingly run covert assaults, data gathering, information theft and subversive activities on behalf of the sponsor nation.

This can include activities pertaining to counterintelligence by detecting and nullifying information theft by means of HUMINT or another method employed by an adversary.

SIGINT

SIGINT or signals intelligence comes in next in the list of intelligence- gathering disciplines.

SIGINT can also be called 'intercept intelligence'. That what began as the interception of messages carried by messenger horsemen between kingdoms and army camps has evolved, too, with the evolution of communication mediums, into SIGINT in contemporary times. COMINT, communication intelligence, and ELINT, or electronic intelligence, through tracking of electronic presence trackers and detection of radar and other signal emitters, are sub-disciplines of SIGINT. They give indications of enemy activities in the media realm and the communication spectrums. SIGINT and COMINT have become the most important mode for large-scale data gathering and general surveillance for security agencies across the world. The internet and the social media explosion have only added to their relevance at the present time.

IMINT

IMINT pertains to intelligence collection using imagery analysis. Imagery includes representations of objects reproduced electronically or by optical means on film, electronic display devices, or other media. IMINT can include video surveillance within a nation's own boundaries, to track the ins-and-outs of suspicious individuals or uprisings and illegal assembly of people that might pose a threat to the nation.

At one time, the imagery intelligence threat was largely restricted to the former Soviet Union and later to the Russian Federation. This is no longer true. The proliferation of space-based imagery systems permits a much greater use of imagery products by nations that previously did not have access to them.

Currently, imagery can be purchased from a variety of sensors. Many developed countries are selling one-metre or better imagery from their space-based reconnaissance systems. The commercial imagery market is likely to continue to grow at an exponential rate, and additional collection systems are currently being developed. One-metre imagery is sufficient to conduct technical analysis of terrain, determine key facilities in an urban area, and conduct detailed analyses of industrial facilities. An additional factor that must be considered is the growing availability of sophisticated imagery workstations and analytical tools. These capabilities will allow adversaries to conduct in-depth analysis for targeting and technical intelligence gathering.

The Open Skies treaty, which was brought into full force in early 2002 and currently has over 35 party states, establishes a regime of unarmed aerial observation flights over the entire territory of its signatories. Originally an idea from the fifties, it was initially an understanding within the members of NATO and the former Warsaw Pact as a means to promote openness and transparency of military forces and activities.

Observation and imagery capture can be done at various ground resolutions of 50 centimetres or less and provide significant detailed information for an imagery analyst. Using the imagery derived from Open Skies flights analysts will be able to identify particular types of equipment by type and capability, and perform detailed analyses of rail, port, industrial, and military facilities.

India is not yet a member state of the treaty, but this highlights how, while the world opening up can promote trust, it must at the same time be cautiously watched from a counter-intelligence viewpoint.

Imagery provides significant benefits to an adversary collecting intelligence against a target nation. First, properly captured imagery can provide geolocation accurately for weapons systems targeting or other intelligence collection platforms. Second, imagery allows activity to be detected, target characteristics studied in detail, and equipment and facilities enumerated. Third, large areas can be covered by imagery sensors for mapping of areas of key importance.

CYBINT

Foreign intelligence services in the new age have been using computer hackers to obtain proprietary data or sensitive government information and have developed the capability to use computer intrusion techniques to disrupt critical infrastructure such as power distribution meshes as well as telecommunication networks. Probably the first known incident was the KGB-sponsored computer intrusion activities by the Hannover Hacker, who was able to access at least 28 government computer systems and steal data in 1986. The KGB was involved in similar efforts with other hacker groups and could have been the earliest sponsors for hacking using malicious code. In the modern world, it's just not hacking computers for foreign intelligence. The internet in today's world has entered into every home, is used for almost every word spoken, for recording every piece of personal information, for every plan, for the distribution of every doctrine, every piece of propaganda. Just about everything leaves its signature in today's internet realm. Listening constantly to this realm all by itself provides valuable intelligence to collectors.

Intelligence Bureau: Structure and Operations

INTELLIGENCE BUREAU: EVOLUTION AND CONSTITUTION

The evolution of modern-day intelligence operations in India

India has a number of intelligence agencies, of which the best known are the IB and the Research and Analysis Wing. Other agencies are Central Bureau of Investigation (CBI), Aviation Research Centre (ARC), Directorate of Enforcement, Directorate of Military Intelligence, Directorate of Naval Intelligence, Directorate of Income Tax, Directorate of Revenue Intelligence, Narcotics Control Bureau (NCB), National Investigation Agency (NIA), National Technical Research Organisation (NTRO), Serious Fraud Investigation Office and many others.

The Intelligence Bureau (IB) is India's prime intelligence agency, said to be the oldest intelligence agency in the world (founded as the Central Special Branch by the Secretary of State for India in London). It has an annual budget of nearly Rs 1900 crore, besides the secret operational funds given by the Government of India from time to time.

The history of India's modern intelligence system goes back to 1885, when then Major General Charles Macgregor was appointed as Quartermaster General and head of the Intelligence department of the British Indian Army in Shimla. The objective was to monitor Russian army deployment in Afghanistan, fearing a Russian invasion into British India through the northwest.

The IB was originally established on December 23, 1887, by the British Secretary of State.

In 1909, the Indian Political Intelligence Office was established in England in response to the developments in Indian revolutionary activities against British rule and this came to be called Indian Political Intelligence (IPI) in 1921. This was a state-run surveillance and monitoring agency in the Indian Office, and it reported to the Secretary of the Public and Judicial Department of the Indian Office and the Director of Intelligence Bureau (DIB) on the Indian mainland, which was in close contact with Scotland Yard and MI5.

After the bifurcation of India in 1947, the then central intelligence system was divided, and one part went to Pakistan. This was also known as Pak IB, which later assumed the name PIB and then ISI (Inter-Services Intelligence), for internal and external intelligence operations.

Over the years, the IB has represented continuity and evolution. It has responded to the changing requirements of the times, maintaining the highest standards of professional excellence. It has undergone structural changes without losing its essential character of an intelligence agency, working to secure the nation against threats, both external and internal. The changing nature of threats has made it imperative for the department to keep pace with the times, to handle its ever-growing responsibilities. It has fashioned appropriate responses to new threats by creating additional capacities and providing the kernel for the formation of new security agencies as and when required. Over time, it proved itself the eyes and ears of the Government of India, though it has never been assigned any executive functions.

The IB faced its worst test in the immediate period after Independence, as its strength decreased drastically, mainly due to British officers leaving India and many others opting to go to the newly formed Pakistan. The threats ranged from unrest fomented by Pak-sponsored elements in Jammu and Kashmir to insurgencies in the north-eastern states. The Intelligence Bureau responded professionally by evolving a sound organisation that met the intelligence and security requirements of the country and proved its mettle during the period of the integration of princely states and language disturbances in the 1950s.

With Independence, the IB quickly developed capacities in the domain of counterintelligence and the collection of foreign intelligence. It was formally divided in September 1968 and the Research and Analysis Wing (RAW) emerged for foreign intelligence.

Structure of the IB

When the British left, the first Indian DIB, the late T. G. Sanjeev Pillai, took over as the first Indian to lead the IB in

1947. He was followed by the more than 27 DIBs till today. The list of DIBs is as follows:

1. T. G. Sanjeev Pillai—12 April 1947—14 July 1950

2. B. N. Mallik—15 July 1950—9 October 1964

3. S. P. Verma—10 October 1964—January 1968

4. M. M. L. Hooja—January 1968—November 1971

5. Atma Jayaram—November 1971—August 1975

6. S. N. Mathur—August 1975—February 1980

7. T.V. Rajeshwar—February 1980—August 1983

8. R. K. Kapoor—August 1983—November 1984

9. H.A. Barari—November 1984—March 1987

10. M. K. Narayanan—April 1987—December 1989

11. R.P. Joshi—December 1989—December 1990

12. M.K. Narayanan—January 1991—February 1992

13. V.G. Vaidya—March 1992—July 1994

14. D.C. Pathak—August 1994—August 1996

15. Abhijeet Mitra—August 1996—September 1996

16. Arun Bhagat—September 1996—April 1998

17. Shyamal Dutta—April 1998—May 2001

18. K. P. Singh—May 2001—July 2004

19. Ajit Doval—July 2004—January 2005

20. E. S. L. Narasimhan—February 2005—December 2006

21. P.C. Halder—Jan 2007—December 2008

22. Rajeev Mathur—January 2009—December 2010

23. N. Sandhu—January 2010—December 2012

24. Syed Asif Ebrahim—1, January 2013—31 December 2014

25. Dineshwar Sharma—January 2015—31 December 2016

26. Rajiv Jain—January 2017 - 2019

27. Aravind Kumar - 2019 onwards

It is said that the IB's failure to provide advanced information about the Sino-Indian War of 1962 and, later, about the India-Pak War in 1965, led to the formation of RAW (Research and Analysis Wing). However, the area in which the Intelligence Bureau consistently delivered excellent results was the steady flow of high-grade intelligence pertaining to the insurgent movements, especially in the North East. The outstanding work done by IB officials in these states made it possible for the security forces to contain the separatist elements. A very significant contribution of the IB ensured that the organisation continuously enjoyed a very high degree of credibility and this undoubtedly was the result of professionalism of highest order.

The IB has a lot of success to its credit, though its operations, being highly secret, are classified and not for public consumption. Due to the extreme secrecy surrounding the agency in operational matters, any disclosure will put the government in an embarrassing position and the lives of its officers at great risk. In addition to the collection of domestic intelligence, the IB is tasked with intelligence operations in border areas, following the 1951 recommendation of the Himmat Singhji Committee also known as North and Northeast Border Committee. In short, all spheres of human activity within India and the neighbouring countries are allocated to the chartered duties of the IB. Understanding the shadow workings of the IB, even members of the IO's family are unaware of the whereabouts of the IB and none of the IOs reveal any operational matters to family members or any other person except to those who are authorised. The IB has multiple tasks, and every government, irrespective of party politics, needs the help of the IB to sustain itself and to take action on various activities both internal and external.

As someone rightly pointed out, the jurisdiction of the IB is anything under the sun. For every national and international activity that has a bearing on national security, IB clearance is sought. For example, to obtain broadcasting rights, to launch an airline, for appointments to all constitutional posts, including judges of the higher courts, Padma Awards, FCRA (Foreign Contribution Regulation Act) Registration grants for any Indian organisations, etc. It has a full-fledged FCRA wing. Other important assignments of the IB are VVIP security, industrial security, airport immigration, visa control for foreigners, anti-terrorism, anti-religious fundamentalism and keeping an eye on all political parties, including the ruling parties. It has a full-fledged wing known as the Bureau of Immigration with Foreigner's Registration Officers in every state and so on. Every government depends upon the IB to have its final say.

The IB Director used to brief the Prime Minister every day, but since the emergence of the role of National Security Advisor in 1998 during the regime of the late Shri A. B. Vajpayee as PM, it is the NSA that is the primary advisor to the PM in national and international security.

During the time of Shri Narendra Modi as PM, in 2018, the position of the NSA was elevated to that of the highest-level bureaucrats in the country. The NSA coordinates all intelligence activities, including military intelligence and state intelligence, and reports to the PM. The NSA is known as the most powerful officer in the bureaucracy and he advises the PM on all internal and external security threats to the country and overseas strategic issues. The NSA also serves as the PM's special envoy on border issues with neighbouring countries and frequently accompanies the PM on his foreign visits. He also coordinates and cooperates with the intelligence agencies of major countries.

Shri Brijesh Mishra, an Indian Foreign Service officer, was the first NSA of India, succeeded by the late J. N. Dixit, another IFS officer. In January 2005, his sudden death paved the way for former Director of the IB Shri M. K. Narayanan, and he continued till January 2010. Then came Shri Shivshankar Menon, another IFS officer, who was in office till May 2014. The NSA as of 2019, Shri Ajit Doval, a former DIB, is a well-known intelligence operational expert throughout the world. The PM depends on him to take any important decisions and make appointments in almost all top posts, such as governors, chiefs of the Army, Navy and Air Force, all heads of paramilitary and Central Police Organisations (CPOs), heads of the IB, RAW and all constitutional authorities.

The symbiotic relationship between the IB and the state police forces provides valuable passing of information essential for the maintenance of public order, particularly in preventing large-scale disturbances and discontent among groups on linguistic, religion, caste and ideology.

Another extremely important sphere of the work of the IB relates to counterterrorism. The growth of terrorism in Punjab and the demand for a separate Khalistan in the 1980s presented a new challenge for security and intelligence agencies. The IB was able to quickly adapt to the change in circumstances and the operatives mastered the art of collecting information in an extremely hostile condition. The growth of Islamic fundamentalism and the use of terrorism as an instrument of state policy by Pakistan have also stretched the capacities of the IB, requiring it to evolve new operational methodologies.

The IB was required to attend to the issue of civil aviation security after the first hijacking of an Indian aircraft in 1971. It set up a dedicated unit to collect intelligence related to civil aviation security and conducted many inspections and sensitisation programs till a formal civil aviation security organisation named the Bureau of Civil Aviation Security was formed. In a similar fashion, the IB ensures the security of vulnerable industrial units and has a special unit for industrial security.

Though it may not be logical to equate the pyramid edifice of the IB with police ranks as the IB is not a police department, practically it is structured according to police lines and hence the ranks are as follows:

Ranks and insignias

- Director of Intelligence Bureau (DIB) - A four-star officer who is considered the senior-most Police Officer of the country and who chairs the All India DGPs' Conference.

- Special Director (DGP)

♦ Additional Director General of Police (ADGP)

♦ Joint Director (Inspector General of Police)

♦ Deputy Director - Deputy Inspector General

♦ Jt. Dy. Director/Asst. Director (Senior/Supdt. of Police)

♦ Deputy Central Intelligence Officer (Addl. Supdt. of Police)

♦ Asst. Central Intelligence Officer - 1 (Deputy Supdt. of Police)

♦ Assistant Central Intelligence Officer - (Inspector)

♦ Junior Intelligence Officer - I (Sub Inspector)

♦ Junior Intelligence Officer - II (Asst. Sub Inspector)

♦ Security Assistant (Head Constable)

Source: Wikipedia

Besides the executive posts, there are various other posts such as ministerial, entrusted with accounts and establishment matters, and technical officers, dealing with all technical operations and other subordinate staff.

OPERATIONAL MATTERS

The operational secrets of any intelligence organisation can never be disclosed even at the cost of one's life. Every government-sponsored intelligence setup is primarily meant to collect the required information and feed it to the required persons, specifically the Prime Minister who is the Chief Executive, as far as India is concerned, either directly or indirectly. Now it is through the National Security Advisor (NSA). No sensitive intelligence reports are debated or even argued in a court of law. Even the honourable judges know that all information cannot be transparent, and some must be hidden in the overall interest of the nation. In the rarest of rare cases, a High Court or a Supreme Court can have an in-camera meeting with the concerned intelligence officer. There are ample examples of these in India despite the fact that several Public Interest Litigations (PILs) have been filed.

Though the CBI, a sister organisation of the IB, wanted to prosecute IB officers in the infamous shootout of a young couple in Gujarat a few years ago, so far nothing has happened. Certain people and organisations, including political parties, continue their hue and cry in the case of an accused in several bomb blast cases who has been held in jail for many years. The learned judges know very well that certain secrets cannot be disclosed for public consumption as they have a bearing on national security.

In secrecy, the IB is used to garner intelligence within India and execute counterintelligence and counterterrorism tasks. Unfortunately, many analysts in India interpret the intelligence data according to the possible liking of their masters to win over the latter's favour, which is highly objectionable and against the principle of professionalism. There are various methods of tradecraft, depending on the given situation and also taking into account the limitations and constraints prevailing in that particular situation.

The main tradecraft techniques are surveillance or shadowing, agent running, secret and open enquiries, checking of available records, using of technical gadgets, interception and monitoring, besides spreading misinformation. Advanced technology in modern times has indeed changed the tradecraft from the conventional method of collecting intelligence. However, the method of technical intelligence has more risk factors as the enemy could creep into the system, either to counter or to nullify efforts.

During the Endowment lecture of the IB 2019, Home Minister of India, Shri Amit Shah, reiterated the government's focus to completely wipe out terrorism, Naxalism and left-wing insurgencies in the next five years.*

This is an audacious target set for the department by the Home Minister and cements the department's cognisance of the renewed intent on the part of the government.

The Minister pointed to the interlinked challenges of human and weapons trafficking, cross-border infiltration, fake Indian currency notes, hawala transactions, drug trafficking as well as cyber threats. He emphasised the need for a special initiative to tackle these challenges.*

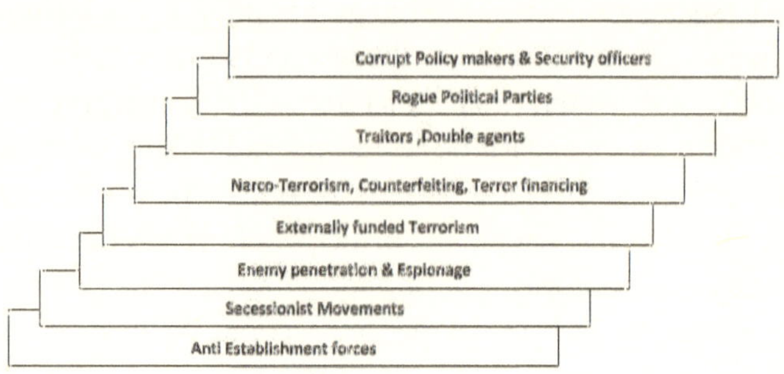

In 2018, the government had already set the wheels in motion by envisioning an entirely new model for the nation's security architecture. It recognised the various avenues that posed a threat to national security. The threats of the current times aren't necessarily the same as from, say, two decades ago.

*Article in The Tribune, 24 December 2019.

It created a new-look Strategic Policy Group headed by the National Security Advisor, Mr. Ajit Kumar Doval, thereby making Doval India's all-powerful security boss. The government also extended the powers of the intelligence agency to monitor even the personal telephonic and internet communications in view of the anti-India propaganda by enemy groups. The nation's Intelligence faculties have been made as potent as ever by these initiatives, but the enemy threats and the various avenues it creeps in through have also adapted over time and this prompts the need for continuous improvement. Threat studies should be a discipline in itself and this should become a continuous endeavour. Studying historic and contemporary international security scenarios and correlating them to the Indian context can be very effective, now more than ever when, thanks to the ever-connecting world, India's problems are no longer very different from the rest of the world. Security threat elements are generally inspired, controlled or spawned by outside mentors. All this warrants a holistic look at what is happening around the world in other countries. What are the security threats they face or have faced in recent times? Do case studies on how can those threat vectors mutate and replicate in India ask whether the strategies they used can be reproduced in India's social communal climate? What can be achieved by an adversary by operating in the shadows? What has worked and what has not?

Security analysis is all about what-if scenarios. But before we do that, we should have a good understanding of the shadow games that get played around.

National Security Threats and Intelligence Operations: The Shadow Games

FIVE

TRANS-BORDER INTELLIGENCE

India shares borders with China, Pakistan, Nepal, Bhutan, Bangladesh and Myanmar in the north and northeast. Similarly, Sri Lanka is near India in the south. So, it is imperative to have a full-fledged and effective intelligence setup along the borders. The entire border is covered by Indian check-posts with a check-post officer in-charge, to monitor the activities across the border and report matters of importance to the government to enable the government to take suitable action by giving the necessary instructions to the defence forces and paramilitary organisations, as the case may be. The army posts are behind the above check-post on the long Chinese border, as per the earlier Colombo plan.

Troop movements, the construction of roads and buildings and any other activities of interest across the border are to be reported. Besides, the movements of inhabitants from one country to another, for grazing cattle, for the collection of firewood and trade between border villages, mostly through the barter system. The mood and temper, disgruntlement and social activities of locals are also monitored by the check-post officers, who are from the intelligence background. They perform the duties of customs, immigration and welfare activities for locals, who are mostly tribal. The reporting and assessment of the check-post officer is more or less accepted by the government and the concerned authorities, over and above the information provided by the other agencies, as the report of the intelligence officer is considered more authentic. Army and paramilitary officers on the borders are also in touch with the check-post officers on various issues that require instant action on security issues.

Nearly 95 percent of all the border check-posts, particularly in the Leh-Ladakh areas, are situated in far-flung mountainous and snow-clad regions. The Check-post Officer and a small contingent most often live in underground bunkers. The land route that is needed for food supply is usually inaccessible for 4 to 5 months owing to heavy snowfall in the region.

The high-altitude areas of the Ladakh region and the Northeast are situated at an altitude of over 16,000 feet, where oxygen is much lower than normal and hence only certain people from the mainland can stay there and some people have to be evacuated due to breathing problems. In fact, thorough medical check-ups are conducted before posting officials to such difficult areas. Despite all these precautions, there are instances of casualties and emergencies at times. In certain check-posts, packed food, kerosene for heating and other day-to-day essentials are supplied through para-dropping by Air Force planes and helicopters. Sometimes, it might take days together for rescue operations to reach these areas due to adverse weather conditions. The temperature goes down to minus 30 degrees centigrade, so in order to keep the staff warm, the necessary warm clothing and the kerosene used for heating the bunkers are supplied.

Many of the check-posts, particularly in the Ladakh area, are inaccessible by roads even in summer and hence mules, donkeys and yaks are the main sources of transport to bring the essentials. A yak (which looks like buffalo and has long hair over its entire body) is suitable for negotiating three to four feet of snow on the track en route. Two or three years is the normal period of posting in such difficult areas, as, for mainlanders, the adverse weather and terrain would affect their health.

These are all some of the difficulties faced by the field officers in border areas, while the obstacles on the plains are indeed different. The Governor of Arunachal Pradesh once commented that Indians know more about the United States than they do about the Northeast. It is true in the case of Ladakh, too.

Terrorists and their handlers change the frequencies of their wireless communications from time to time, making it difficult for intelligence agencies to monitor and decipher the messages. According to ground forces in J&K, the abrogation of Article 370 of the Indian constitution, followed by restrictions imposed on the internet and other stringent measures, Pakistan-backed terrorist outfits were said to have switched over to a new system for communication. Ground sources said that the LeT had been tasked with carrying out further attacks on security forces.

According to a report, all the electronic monitors of the Indian Army along the Pakistan border were defunct for unknown reasons for nearly two months in the last quarter of 2019, affecting intelligence operations. There were apparent alerts in the high echelons of the government over this alarming development. The government was particularly anxious that messages were being sent to militants in the valley from across.

Since nearly ninety percent of transborder intelligence is received through technical gadgets, it was tough for all intelligence agencies, including the IB and Army intelligence, operating on the borders to communicate with their agents across the border. This situation necessitated that all security agencies revive their technical support wings and launch special operations in enemy territory, including infiltration and planting.

Within a short span of a few days after an Indian infantry battalion convoy was ambushed on the Manipur border with Myanmar, the Indian Army launched two transborder surgical strikes to neutralize the Naga and Manipuri extremists responsible for the attack. The base camps of insurgents belong to one outfit of the NSCN(K), led by Khaplang, and Kanglein Yawol Kapna Loop (KYKL), a militant outfit from Tripura, and targeted the Sagaing division of Myanmar. A joint operation was mounted by India's elite special forces and was meticulously planned and executed. These retaliatory counterattacks were carried out based on hard intelligence collected and collated by multiple HUMINT (human intelligence) and electronic surveillance sources.

India and its immediate neighbour Nepal, which also borders China, pledged to enhance border security with intelligence sharing, including on transborder crimes. It was mutually agreed to continue holding regular coordination meetings to handle many border issues, including security, human trafficking, transborder crimes, the smuggling of narcotics and weaponry, through timely intelligence sharing between both countries. Nepal is strategically important and vulnerable for India due to its geographical position. Similarly, Nepal also wants India's help as it has looked at China with suspicion ever since the annexation of Tibet. Nepal, as a matter of fact, is always apprehensive about problems from China as it is aware of the Chinese ambition for territorial expansion.

After the annexation of Tibet by China, the Dalai Lama and some of his followers crossed over to India via the northeast border. During 1972-73, on the Ladakh borders, the check-post officer at the tri-junction post in the northern sector of Ladakh noticed some electronic devices on a series of poles erected on the Line of Actual Control (LAC). While on a reconnaissance trip, the daredevil officer somehow managed to remove one of these poles with the device fitted at its top and physically lifted it without the army on the other side noticing.

He then brought it to a check-post nearly 2 kilometres from the LAC. He sent a coded wireless message, (that was the only form of communication at that time) to Leh headquarters, from where it was transmitted to the IB HQ in Delhi. Specialists in Delhi analysed the information and instructed him to wait before further action.

Within a week, a message from Delhi said that a three-member team from a foreign intelligence agency from a friendly country would be arriving at Leh airport with certain equipment in an ARC AN12 aircraft. The officer in charge of logistics at the IB in Leh received the foreign agents at the airport with suitable cover and alibis to avoid attention from army personnel and local labourers in the airport. The foreign agents were brought to the officer's mess in Leh. When asked about food and water, the agents replied that they would not require anything as they had brought everything they needed for a week. The agents even rejected the use of our bed sheets, blankets and other warm clothes till they returned to Delhi on the third day to report. The agents had everything needed for a week's supply carried in their rucksacks, and even wore local Ladakhi attire when moving about for the sake of camouflage.

This was the degree of security consciousness, secrecy and mutual suspicion among spies, even when working together on the same mission.

The next morning, the foreign agents were airlifted by an Indian air force chopper to the check-post, took over the suspicious device and later boarded the ARC flight back to Delhi. It should be mentioned that China was a closed country at that time without outside contacts, and the free world was eagerly monitoring every bit of information about the communist regime.

The IO reporting observations is not necessarily aware of how the information is used. Further decisions on using the information are always made by the Centre and separate officers take it ahead from there. The reporting IO is not necessarily kept in the know.

Even when Delhi is driving the mission, it doesn't mean that Indian IOs will be always be at the top of the knowledge chain. Knowledge is always on a need-to-know-basis. The IOs at Leh who detected the devices facilitated the agents' visit and the delivery of the device to Delhi, but never knew how the episode ended.

Transborder intelligence is something that usually gets shared with friendly agencies abroad and information and help are given back as well. There is a great degree of mistrust between any two intelligence agencies from different countries, even when their heads of state are seen shaking hands and confirming in front of the cameras how deep-rooted their countries' friendship is. Nevertheless, the thumb rule is that my enemy's enemy is a friend. Hence when it comes to transborder intelligence ops, like-minded nations with suspicions about a common target cooperate, and sometimes depute their IOs under the other country's central command and provide gadgets and other support as well.

SIX

POLITICAL PARTIES

Compared with other democratic countries, India has perhaps the largest number of political parties (now estimated to be more than 200) formed after independence. Every ruling government seeks the IB's reports on the activities of political parties, including the party or parties in the government itself, in order to survive and to take counteractions.

It may be noted that immediately after the 2018 bye-elections, when the opposition performed better than the ruling party and its alliance, top functionaries of the government asked the IB to prepare and submit detailed reports on the mood and temper of voters ahead of the 2019 General Election. Besides, the top government functionaries were also asked to analyse the inputs already provided by the IB to see where the ruling parties went wrong and build up case studies for the upcoming elections. According to sources, the IB gave the ruling government information about the growing unpopularity of the then Chief Minister six Rajasthan and the possible tendency to anti-incumbency in both Madhya Pradesh and Chhattisgarh. The report also mentioned that rural distress, particularly among the marginal agriculturists, and the unemployment among the youth were likely to go against the government. This led to introspection among the leaders of the ruling party and they started charting out the necessary strategy to ease the situation in all states, ultimately leading to the declaration of various popular schemes for the general public just before the 2019 elections were declared.

India stands among the first in political corruption. Political corruption is the use of power or a network of contacts among public and government officials to amass wealth through illegal activities both for personal gain or for a political party. Criminalisation of politics has become the order of the day. Nearly one-third of the MPs in Parliament, i.e. 158 out of 543, faced criminal charges. According to the Association of Democratic Reforms, a political watchdog, 1448 out of the 4835 candidates contesting the 2014 election, per their own affidavits filed with the Election Commission of India, faced criminal charges for heinous crimes such as rape, extortion, murder, attempt to murder, kidnapping and robbery, among other things. Of these 1448, 98 candidates were fielded by the major political parties and 36 of them won, including seven MPs and 29 state legislators. All these facts point to the public apprehension about whether India's political parties can ever be serious about fighting corruption and the criminalisation of politics.

It is suspected that many political leaders keep in touch with and protect underworld dons, hardcore criminals, religious fundamentalists and terrorists in order to make money and annihilate political rivals within and outside their parties. We all know of times when some of the most wanted fugitive criminals and terrorists were protected by certain political leaders, undoubtedly for their own and their family security.

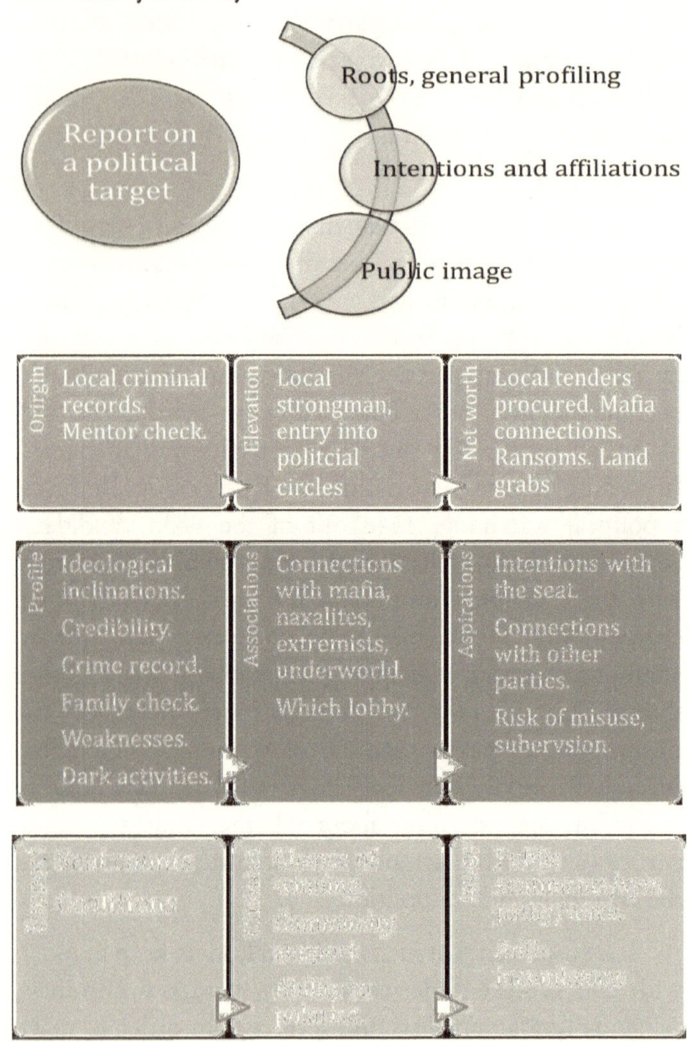

Intelligence officers constantly collect all necessary intelligence needed for national security and relay it to state governments for further action. Though some ruling state governments are reluctant to take action on intelligence inputs, undoubtedly for their personal and party interest, action is inevitable either today or tomorrow. All this makes it necessary that the centre is in full awareness of its own party men as well as other regional parties, their activities, past records, people's perception of their performance as well as any secret affiliations they might have.

It is undeniable that there have been instances wherein certain top officers, both at the states and at the Centre, in order to please their political bosses and to be in their good books for professional prospects and prized postings even after retirement, probably hid vulnerable intelligence procured through hardship and risk by the lower ranks, thereby compromising even the security of the country. In short, the ego factor at times overrules the integrity and basic responsibility of some officers, particularly the deputations from the State Police. One of the most important lacunae when it comes to deputations from the State Police is that some of these officers feed information clandestinely to their state rulers, as they have greater allegiance to the state ruling party, and aim to gain the confidence of the chief ministers rather than serving the interests of the central government that is ruled by a different political party. To cite a fictitious example, an officer who comes to the IB for a short period on deputation comes to know most secrets, including the sources or agents for the department, and this officer can misuse his power and position, creating embarrassment for the directly recruited IB officers and agents.

A few years ago, there were talks of a deputed police officer from a state cadre having brought embarrassment and threats to a permanent officer in the IB who was running a high-level source or agent. The deputed officer, being in a senior position, was able to find out the personal particulars of the source from top-secret records and contacted him directly, compromising the very basic norms of security in agent running. Ultimately, the department lost the source, who was feeding us very valuable information about a militant political party. Luckily, the life of the handling officer was saved. That is the reason why there is an urgent need for the IB to bring people from other state cadres and get them absorbed in the IB in order to create a feeling of belonging to the present department.

The distrust and apprehensions amongst the ruling and opposition political parties

Very often, valuable intelligence has been lost in oblivion with the ever-present slugfest between the Centre and state machineries. While India's federalism, albeit quasi, may be beneficial elsewhere, when it comes to effectively and jointly acting on a valuable piece of intelligence brought out painstakingly by an IO, the rollup to the Centre fails miserably. The federal element was undoubtedly adopted into the constitution by the republic's founders for good reason and it surely helps regulate and curtail the degree of dominance and subjugation that a central government can impose on states that may not necessarily wish to adopt each and every one of the central party's points of doctrine.

But we need to understand that the states form the nation and strategies on national security, while the Centre's prerogative needs to be executed at the state level. The threat to the nation's security that needs to be neutralized can be a state element!

Three of the major hurdles in this respect are:

A. The dependency on the state machinery to invoke the state police and act on the Centre's intelligence inputs to them. The information has to pass the state's litmus test on whether it subverts the state's own interests in any way. This leads to cherry picking by the state from all of the available leads.

B. Deputations from state cadres to central departments like the IB muddy the water even more. These deputed officers work for a certain number of years in the bureau only to go back to their masters in the state government afterwards. This practice, right at the face of it, presents itself as the perfect recipe for pandemonium and confusion over the allegiance of the officer. Should his loyalty be to the Centre or the centre-owned bureau, when he is planning to head back? What was the purpose of his little foray into the kernel of the Centre's intelligence? Even the officer himself is confused sometimes.

C. What if the persons or groups on whom the Centre wants to conduct surveillance are the state's ruling party itself or its coalition?

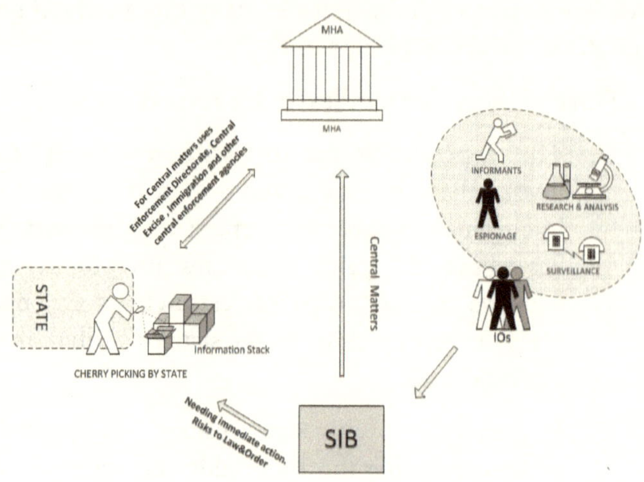

Sometimes, the sneaking goes beyond individuals or businesses or NGOs. Sometimes it's yet another political party who is the target.

While this might raise a few eyebrows, this has always been in practice and there is nothing wrong with it. The intelligence bureau is a centre-owned instrument for gathering knowledge and overseeing everything and is bestowed on the Centre when a government is democratically elected. It's like how the nation's defence faculties are completely the Centre's prerogative, to be used for what it is meant for. Not to use it when needed would actually make the ruling administration culpable of the crime of inaction in the face of an assault on the nation.

In the same way, if the Centre feels that intelligence gathering on the ins and outs of a political party is in the nation's interest, it should proceed with it. That is its duty towards the nation. This was more relevant in the 1970s and 80s, a time of paranoid or even rogue political parties, Marxists, Maoists and extremists, gaining arms and support, and working at the behest of external powers. When the opposition's feeling of vulnerability before an ever-more-powerful elected government surpasses sense, it can devise plans to topple the government un-electorally, even if it meant colluding with the nation's enemies, to create chaos, terror or even stoke an armed rebellion against the establishment.

Back in the 1980s, a militant political party was holding its national conference. Its internal deliberations and decisions were to be covered clandestinely by the IB using technical gadgets. A technical team from Delhi arrived two days before the conference to study and assess the actual field situation, including spots to be selected for the installation of technical devices, besides a safe house for monitoring and recording the proceedings. One of the technical officers was accompanied by an SIB IO and went to the main function ground which was already fenced off. There were policemen on guard duty at the main entrance, with uniformed party volunteers. The podium was about to be completed and the IOs went undercover as electricity board employees to check supply lines. While one of the SIB IO was talking to a party volunteer near the podium and engaging him to divert his attention, another colleague went underneath the podium to place a device and came out without giving rise to any suspicion, displaying his exemplary skills at stealth.

Similarly, three more devices were placed under tables in the hotel rooms of top party leaders. Hoodwinking the manager of the hotel under the cover of checking security, the IOs entered the room and did their job. Then came the most difficult part of monitoring, for which mobile surveillance was organised near the hotel and a room of a nearby house was taken on rent. The landlord, who got suspicious regarding the large-sized wireless receiver machines being carried into his apartment, was taken into confidence with assurances for a quick resolution to a pension-related issue of his that had been stuck in limbo for years*. All the deliberations were thus recorded each day and when the meeting ended, the recordings were heard and put in black and white to transmit to the Delhi office.

The team deputed for mobile monitoring near the guest house did their job during the night hours and in the mornings, when the leaders were in their rooms before they left for the main delegate sessions. The agents of the government would thus infiltrate into just about anything and carry the information back to the Centre. New Delhi demanded to know and the IB would make it happen. The IOs are agnostic to the 'who' and the 'why'. Nothing was and should be allowed so much obscurity and privacy that the nefarious and the scheming elements feel so unbridled and powerful.

*Incidentally, one of the IOs ran into him years later, his pension was still stuck.

SEVEN

RELIGIOUS FUNDAMENTALISM

Terrorism is the deliberate and indiscriminate use of violence as a medium to invoke fear among the masses, panic in the government and pandemonium within the security institutions, in order to create a climate of fear and civil unrest, with an end goal of disrupting the ethnic, religious or the political fabric of a region. It is used in this regard primarily to refer to violence during peace time or in war against known combatants.

Terrorists could carry out attacks at any time, for which a vigilant intelligence system is necessary to take timely and apt actions to counter the terrorists. Terrorism in India, according to the Home Ministry, poses a significant threat to the peace and tranquillity of the country. It has become a universal phenomenon and India is perhaps the worst affected. As per the Home Ministry, the following are the major terrorist attacks since 1980 and terrorism has claimed a total of more than 7000 lives and left over 3200 injured.

The list of terror attacks in India, provided at the end of this chapter, gives a bird's eye view of the continuous terrorist attacks not only by religious extremists but also by Naxalites. Our unsung heroes in the IB thwarted five major attacks ahead of Republic Day 2019 and helped the country have a very happy Republic Day. Many of our nation's honoured personnel are overtly acknowledged on the Republic Day, but the people who quietly work behind the scenes to ensure the safety of the nation are unknown to the general public. They are not out in the open, nor do they appear in the media, but work tirelessly for days to ensure that people can sleep in peace. Thanks to their constant surveillance, constant listening, while spending their entire life in the shadows, staring at greyness and making sense out of randomness, IB officers continuingly neutralise threat vectors and thwart assaults on the nation and its people.

The first was in Punjab, where there was movement of terrorists from Khalistan coming together with terrorists from Jammu and Kashmir to carry out attacks in both Punjab and New Delhi. Zakir Musa, who entered Punjab in the disguise of a Sikh, was planning on carrying out a strike in Ludhiana along with a Khalistan terrorist. He was in touch with persons from the local module.

In December 2018, the National Investigation Agency, acting on the basis of several inputs provided by the IB, raided the hideouts of modules both in Delhi and Uttar Pradesh, which led to the arrest of more than ten persons. The IB had reported that the ISI had been setting up modules in the name of ISIS in India, in order to disrupt Republic Day and embarrass the security agency.

Similarly, Abdul Latif, alias Dilawar, was arrested by the Delhi police on the night of January 19, 2019, following a tip-off that JeM terrorists were masterminding terror strikes in Delhi during the Republic Day celebrations. Incriminating materials were recovered from Dilawar. The Maharashtra Anti-Terrorist squad arrested seven persons and unearthed incriminating materials following the intelligence inputs. They were believed to be planning on carrying out an acid and knife attack and were inspired by the Islamic State.

Ever since the Babri Masjid was demolished in 1992, the communal atmosphere in India has been disturbing. The insecurity that is felt by a large section of Muslims has added further fuel to the fire and provided a better opportunity for the ISI to exploit the situation. It has been noticed that the ISI has slowly and steadily extended its tentacles in almost all states in India. The Mumbai bomb blasts in March 1993 further proved that the ISI has successfully penetrated areas not only in Punjab and Kashmir but also in Maharashtra and other states. The ISI has managed to systematically subvert the minds of a sizable number of the Muslim community and won over the underworld mafia. This has further complicated the issue and money has become easily available for fundamentalist groups to carry out blasts and create panic among people.

The underworld connected with the extortion and sale of narcotics has been able to recruit several disgruntled, frustrated, unemployed Muslim youth for narco-terrorism. It is a well-known fact that one of the main sources of income for the ISI is from the narcotics trade. There is also reason to believe that the ISI has been printing Indian currency notes, particularly of high denominations, and managing to send across counterfeit currency printed in Nepal and Bangladesh to India not only with the intention of destabilizing the Indian economy but also to lavishly pay their agency in India. One of the major efforts of the ISI is to create distress among various communities and to organize sabotage in major Indian cities.

There are indications that Pakistan, through the ISI, might have developed a very well-organized intelligence mechanism in India by penetrating defence services and other security organisations. There are incidents of defence secrets being passed on to Pakistani intelligence and there are arrests of defence personnel from time to time for alleged links with the LeT, an ISI-sponsored Islamic terrorist outfit functioning from the POK. There are examples where it was detected that Pakistan, with the support of the ISI, got Indian youth infiltrated into the defence forces from the recruitment level onwards, not only at the rank and file level but also as officers. Besides, there have been reports that the ISI, with the help of the underworld, has been able to win over some politicians, including MPs, who started raising the question of Muslims being denied opportunities in government departments, including defence and judiciary, in proportion to the Muslim population.

The latest trend in Islamic terrorism, in the emergence of terrorist acts not only in India but around the world, is the involvement of elite professionals in blasts. The Al Qaeda operatives who perpetrated the 9/11 incident in the US were all trained pilots who were able to fly some of the most advanced jets and the people arrested in connection with the Mumbai train blasts were software professionals, doctors and chemical engineers.

Though the desperation among Muslim youth could be attributed to poverty and unemployment among the

Muslim community, the liberal democracy of modern times, including in India, is being exploited by religious fundamentalist groups. Consumerism, liberalisation and commercialism have piqued people's minds with an unquenchable yearning to gain more. This has prompted the educated unemployed youth to become tools in the hands of the ISI operatives. The prime accused in the Mumbai blasts were qualified Muslims who were unable to get the employment of their choice with the salaries they wanted. The germination of terrorists in economically backward areas is linked to the preparedness to become a 'jihadi' under the guidance of fundamentalist organisations like the Student Islamic Movement of India (SIMI) and LeT.

History also shows that the military mercilessly suppressed the Razakars, a terrorist outfit looked after by the Nizam of Hyderabad to oppose the annexation of his kingdom by the Indian union, which included Marathwada. Though all the then members of the Razakars are dead and buried now, their legacy seems to secretly prevail even among sections of Muslims from Beed, Parbhani and Aurangabad in the Marathwada region in Maharashtra. In short, all these factors, combined with growing ghettoization of the Muslim community, provided a fertile ground for SIMI and the LeT to plant the seeds of jihad which was later taken over by ISIS.

All this gets even more threatening when the host nation loses control over the monster it has created. Three decades ago, the Pakistani military created Lashkar-e-Taiba, the group responsible for the 2008 Mumbai terrorist attacks, to take forward its Kashmir agenda and most importantly to inflict wounds on India.

Now Lashkar-e-Taiba has developed an independent support base thanks partly to its charity arm, which runs popular social-welfare and educational programmes. Today, the group's financing is strong, its terrorist capability formidable, and its ideology appealing to many across the country and beyond its borders as well. Over the years, India's diplomacy and the influence it wields with the US and EU have enabled it to polarize the world's opinion with regards to terrorism. The world order now unanimously views these as terrorists more than freedom fighters. The Pakistani establishment is now hard-pressed to control it but is unable to. Personal relationships between Pakistani military officers and members of Lashkar-e-Taiba have also weakened the resolve of the army to confront the group.

Pakistan's predicament with Lashkar-e-Taiba illustrates the risks from terrorists to a sponsoring state as well. Proxy relationships sometimes establish deep rooting of the terrorist organisation into the socio-political fabric of the sponsoring nation as well and the role the organisations play sometimes extends beyond the original use-case for its conception.

Usually by the time its activities either have fulfilled or are no longer desired for a sponsor's tactical or long-term strategic goals, it has gained so much ground and allegiance across sections of the civil society as well as in the military establishment, that it is difficult to get rid of them merely at the back of political will. Hillary Clinton, the then secretary of state, noted in a 2011 press conference with Pakistani Foreign Minister Hina Rabbani Khan, "It's like that old story—you can't keep snakes in your backyard and expect them only to bite your neighbours. Eventually those snakes are going to turn on whoever has them in the backyard."

Front groups: Tools of infiltration and nurseries for new recruits

To gain public credibility, attract new supporters, generate revenue, spawn new offshoots and sleeper cells, and acquire other resources, terrorist and insurgent groups need to undertake activities that are entirely separate from their overtly violent primary activities.

Sometimes this is achieved by infiltrating political parties, labour unions, community groups, and charitable organisations. Operating in the guise of such front groups, which provide a façade of legitimacy which might otherwise be unobtainable, these infiltrators can bolster regional allies, attract mass support, and, most importantly, obtain human recruits in the target nation itself.

Today, groups as diverse as Al Qaeda, the Kurdistan People's Congress (formerly known as the Partiya Karkaren Kurdistan), Lashkar-e-Taiba in Jammu and Kashmir, and the LTTE operate through political, social, and charitable fronts.

Terrorists gain recruits and followers through these front groups, primarily charitable organisations, religious community meetings and missionary conferences.

The Tabhlighi Jamaat (TJ), which entered the public knowledge after the Jamaat's international conference in Delhi in March 2020, to which 400 cases of coronavirus in the country were attributed, is yet another system driver that sustains the working dynamics of many Islamist 'Armed Non-State Actors' across the world. From its very cosmetically designed exterior, it looks like a puritan community with the mission to inculcate true Islamic piety across the "Umma", the global Islamic community. It identifies itself as a non-political, missionary organisation that aims to build an Islamic society based on the teachings of the Koran. The organisation is a century old, initially founded in the Mewat region of then northern India as a small community for faith revival among Muslims, to retain and preserve the tenets of true Islam in a period when the Islamic regimes were on the decline and the Marathas and then later the British had consolidated their grip on India. In reality though, on many occasions, the Jamaat has acted as nursery for indoctrinating Islamist terrorists. It invites idealistic Muslim men into conferences and prayer meetings and thereby provides the needed audience for radical missionaries, many of whom have overlapping membership with jihadist groups, to preach their extremists ideologies.

After the partition of the country, the TJ split into various chapters. There is primarily the Indian chapter, the Pakistani chapter, the Bangladeshi chapter and the Malaysian one. These chapters chose their own paths of varying levels of radicalisation. But once every year, the Jamaat allows for the intermixing of members of these chapters for 40 days in the conferences that it arranges. This acts as the platform for corrupting the minds of young men and converting them into new recruits for anti-national activities.

The externally controlled radical preachers hence prepare their own legion of impassioned young men. These recruits then go back to the mainstream, penetrate into state institutions and await instructions from across the border. This has many significant benefits.

The first is information: Infiltrating organs of the state, particularly the security forces, can help generate invaluable information about the government's capabilities, intentions, and weaknesses. Such infiltration, therefore, might be considered a form of intelligence collection against the state.

Second, penetration can give terrorists and insurgents opportunities to plant false information, redirect the state's potentially lethal gaze, force the authorities to misallocate resources, and otherwise derail the state's campaign. This too is a type of intelligence operation; like counterintelligence carried out by government intelligence services, it (secretly) aims to disrupt the organisation and operations of enemy forces.

Third, successful infiltration may lead to opportunities to steal government funds, weapons, equipment, and other resources.

Just as infiltrators can help derail the state's counterterrorist or counterinsurgency campaigns, so too can they degrade the state's ability to provide key public services by misdirecting resources, stealing funds, and spreading false and divisive rumours among those in the government workforce.

Infiltration of government institutions has been a tactic of revolutionaries through history. In Bangladesh, the radical Jamaat-e-Islami party, which sponsors a network of 15,000 guerrillas, has filled the country's armed forces, security services, and civilian agencies with its sympathizers. Although, it must be mentioned that insurgent infiltration is not limited to state institutions; insurgents have systematically penetrated universities, where they reportedly occupy top academic and administrative positions.

The following is the list of major terrorist incidents in India since June 1980.

Date	Incident	Location	Persons dead	Persons injured
June 8, 1980[TP1]	Mandai Massacre	Tripura	400	-
August 2, 1984	Meenambakkam Bomb Blast	Tamil Nadu	30	25
July 7 1987	Haryana Killings	Haryana	36	60
May 21, 1991	Assassination of Rajiv Gandhi	Tamil Nadu	15	20+
June 15, 1991	Punjab Killings	Punjab	126	200
October 17, 1991	Rudrapur Bombings	Uttarakhand	41	140
March 12, 1993	Mumbai Bombings	Mumbai	257	700+
April 9, 1993	Palar Blast	Karnataka	22	13
August 8, 1993	Bombing of RSS Office in Chennai	Tamil Nadu	11	7
December 30, 1996	Brahmaputra Mail Train Bombing	Assam	33	150
February 14, 1998	Coimbatore Bombings	Tamil Nadu	58	200+
May 20, 2000	Bagber Massacre	Tripura	25	-
May—July 2000	Church Bombings	Karnataka, Goa & Andhra Pradesh	0	Unknown

June 9, 2000	Charar-e-Sharif Mosque Attack	Charari Sharif	4	60
December 22, 2000	Attack on Red Fort	Delhi	3	14
October 1, 2001	J&K Legislative Assembly Car Bombing	Jammu & Kashmir	38	Unknown
December 13, 2001	Parliament Attack, New Delhi	New Delhi	7	18
May 13, 2002	Jaunpur Train Crash	Jaunpur	12	80
March 27, 2002	Raghunath Temple	Jammu	11	20
September 10, 2002	Rafiganj Train Wreck	Bihar	200	150+
November 22, 2002	Raghunath Temple	Jammu	14	45
December 6, 2002	Mumbai Bus Bombing	Mumbai	2	14
December 21, 2002	Kurnool Train Crash	Andhra Pradesh	20	80
September 24, 2002	Attack on Akshardham Temple	Gujarat	31[TP2]	80
January 27, 2003	Mumbai Bombing	Mumbai	1	28
March 13, 2003	Mumbai Train Bombing	Mumbai	10	Unknown
July 28, 2003	Bus Bombing	Mumbai	4	32

Contd,

August 25, 2003	Bombings	Mumbai	52	Unknown
January 2, 2004	Railway Station Attack	Jammu	4	14
August 15, 2004	Dhemaji School Bombing	Assam	18	40
July 5, 2005	Ram Janmabhoomi Attack	Ayodhya, UP	6	-
July 28, 2005	Jaunpur Train Bombing	Jaunpur, UP	13	50
October 29, 2005	Delhi Blast	New Delhi	70	250
December 28, 2005	Indian Institute of Science Shooting	Karnataka	1	4
March 7, 2006	Attacks in different places	Varanasi / UP	21	62
July 11, 2006	Series of 7 train bombings	Mumbai	2009	500+
September 8, 2006	Vicinity of Mosque at Malegaon	Maharashtra	37	125
February 18, 2007	Samjhauta Express train bombing	Haryana	68	50
May 18, 2007	Mecca Masjid Bombing	Hyderabad	13	Unknown
August 25, 2007	Twin blast	Hyderabad	42	54

October 11, 2007	Ajmer Dargah Bombing	Rajasthan	3	17
October 14, 2007	Movie Theatre Blast	Ludhiana / Punjab	6	Unknown
November 24, 2007	Series of Explosions	Lucknow, Varanasi and Faizabad / UP	16	17
January 1, 2008	Rampur Attack by LeT	UP	8	5
May 13, 2008	9 bomb blasts	Jaipur / Rajasthan	63	200+
July 25, 2008	8 Bomb blasts	Bangalore	1	20
July 26, 2008	17 Serial bomb blasts	Ahmedabad / Gujarat	29	110+
September 13, 2008	5 bomb blasts in Delhi Markets	Delhi	33	130
September 27, 2008	Bomb Blast at Mehrauli	Delhi	3	21
September 29, 2008	Bomb Blast	Maharashtra & Gujarat	10	80
October 1, 2008	Bombings	Agartala / Tripura	4	100+
October 21, 2008	Bombing	Imphal	17	40+
October 30, 2008	Bombings	Assam	81	470
November 26, 2008	Mumbai Attacks	Mumbai	171	239

Contd,

January 1, 2009	Guhawati Bombings	Assam	6	67
April 6, 2009	Bombings	Assam	3	31
February 13, 2010	Pune Bombings	Maharashtra	8	30
February 15, 2010	Silda Camp Attack	West Bengal	12	-
April 6, 2010	Maoist Attack	Dantewada / Chhattisgarh	42 including 8 terrorist	8
May 17, 2010	Bus Bombing	Dantewada / Chhattisgarh	15-22	15
May 28, 2010	Jnaneshwari Express Train Derailment	West Bengal	74	100+
December 7, 2010	Bombing	Varanasi / UP	1	20
July 13, 2011	Bombings	Mumbai	6	65
September 7, 2011	Bombings	Delhi	9	38
February 13, 2012	Attack on Israeli Diplomats	Delhi	0	4
August 1, 2012	Bombings	Pune / Maharashtra	0	1
February 21, 2013	Blasts	Hyderabad	8	59
March 13, 2013	Srinagar Attacks	J&K	7	10
April 17, 2013	Bangalore Blasts	Bengaluru	0	16

May 25, 2013	Naxal Attack in Darbha Valley	Chhattisgarh	14	16
June 24, 2013	Srinagar Attack	J&K	4	9
July 7, 2013	Maoist Attack	Dumka / Chhattisgarh	2	-
July 7, 2013	Bodh Gaya Bombings	Bihar	0	5
October 27, 2013	Patna Bombings	Bihar	2	33
December 26, 2013	Jalpaiguri Bombings	West Bengal	5	5
March 11, 2014	Attack	Chhattisgarh	8	3
April 25, 2014	Blast	Jharkhand	8	5
April 28, 2014	Blast in Budgam Dist,	J&K	0	18
May 1, 2014	Chennai Train Bombing	Tamil Nadu	1	14
May 1, 2014	Assam Violence	Assam	33	Unknown
May 12, 2014	Maoist Blast in Gadchiroli Dist.	Maharashtra	7	2
December 23, 2014	Violence	Assam	85	Unknown
December 28, 2014	Bomb Blast at Church Street	Bangalore	1	5
January 23, 2015	Ara Civil Court Bombing	Bihar	2	7+
March 20, 2015	Jammu Attack	J&K	6	10

Contd,

June 4—9, 2015	Manipur Ambush—surgical Strike by Indian Armed Forces near Myanmar—surgical Strike by Indian Armed Forces near Myanmar Border	Manipur	176 including 158 terrorists	15
July 27, 2015	Gurdaspur Attack	Punjab	10	15
January 2, 2016	Attack on Pathankot Air Force Station	Punjab	7	-
June 25, 2016	Pampore Attack	Pampore	8	22
August 5, 2016	Kokrajhar Attack	Assam	14	15
September 18, 2016	Uri Attack—Surgical Strike by Indian Army	J&K	20	8
October 3, 2016	Baramulla Attack	J&K	0	Unknown
October 6, 2016	Attack on Rashtriya Rifles Camp / Handwara	J&K	0	-
November 29, 2016	Nagrota Attack	J&K	10	Unknown
April 24, 2017	Sukma Attack	Chhattisgarh	26	-
March 7, 2017	Ujjain Passenger Train Bombing	Bhopal / MP	0	10

July 11, 2017	Amarnath Yatra Attack	Anantnag, J&K	7	6
February 10, 2018	Sunjuwan Attack	J&K	11	11
March 13, 2018	Sukma Attack	Chhattisgarh	9	
February 14, 2019	Pulwama Attack, Awantipura	J&K	46	250 – 300
March 7, 2019	Bus Stand Blast, Jammu	J&K	3	28 – 35

EIGHT

NARCO-TERRORISM

In terms of the general trade in narcotics and psychotropic substances, India is sandwiched between the two major sources of supply of illicit drugs, namely the 'Golden Crescent' (Pakistan, Afghanistan and Iran) and the 'Golden Triangle' (Myanmar, Thailand and Laos). The Golden Crescent, however, is the main area of concern. This is borne out by the fact that the bulk of heroin seizures (over 35 percent) involved the Golden Crescent; the Golden Triangle accounted for barely 0.65 percent. In addition, while trafficking in cocaine and amphetamines or synthetic drugs continues to engage enforcement agencies, the illicit trade in heroin and hashish continues to be the most problematic area.

In the immediate neighbourhood, Sri Lanka is a major route for the movement of drugs and has witnessed a spurt in the trafficking of heroin. Nearly 40 percent of all Indian seizures of heroin have been on the India–Sri Lanka route and mostly involve Sri Lankan nationals. In Nepal, the main items were *ganja* and *charas*. Nearly 40 percent of *charas* seized in the country is sourced from Nepal.

Myanmar and Thailand have a number of syndicates engaged in the illicit manufacture of synthetic drugs as well as heroin. Precursor chemicals like ephedrine and pseudo-ephedrine are known to be smuggled from India into this region and small quantities of synthetic drugs and heroin are smuggled from Myanmar to India.

In terms of the global drug trade, estimated to be over 10,000 tonnes, India is not a major player either in terms of volume or financial turnover. Besides, it is neither a major source nor a significant destination at present. However, its continuity with the Golden Crescent region gives it substantial potential as a transit route and as a target for narco-terrorism. Conceptually, narco-terrorism has three manifestations: terrorism by narco-trafficking groups; direct sales of drugs by terrorist groups to generate funds; and state patronage to facilitate drug trafficking by narco-gangs. In the Indian context, while the first is virtually non-existent, the second was visible in Punjab. It is the third aspect that has the maximum significance in the present context.

Narco-terrorism of the third variety emerged in the region following the US–Soviet engagement in Afghanistan and in the Indian context it comprises several elements.

India is close to the largest opium production centres in Afghanistan and that provides the source. The ISI and Pakistan army have used drugs to generate money in order to finance the proxy war in India, which provides the motive. Organised crime gangs like Dawood Ibrahim's and others are readily available and have an extensive network and the logistical capability to smuggle drugs and that provides the vehicle. Terrorists, fundamentalists, separatists, subversive and criminal groups that are enlisted by the ISI to serve its strategic objectives require funds for operational and infrastructural expenditure. It provides the main consumers. The convergence of the interests of these elements is the primary engine for narco-terrorism, and this has implications for India's national security.

Recent developments indicate a significant increase in opium cultivation in Afghanistan. Opium is a most lucrative crop and the area under cultivation has increased by more than 60 percent. Consequently, production increased by 17 percent. The availability of undisclosed stocks is estimated at more than 1000 metric tonnes, a significant increase.

In terms of the route, the Iran–Iraq war in the late eighties choked the movement of drugs via Iran. Subsequently, a bulk of heroin consignments moved westwards, either through the Balkans or via CIS countries and Russia. However, with the tightening up of routes through the CIS countries and in Europe, trafficking through India has increased, causing serious security threats. As regards the motive, Nawaz Sharif (the former Prime Minister of Pakistan) himself disclosed years ago that General Aslam Beg (the then Pak Army Chief) and Lieutenant General Mohammad Asad Durrani (the head of Pakistan's intelligence agency) had, in early 1991 itself, proposed a detailed blueprint for selling heroin to pay for the country's covert military operations. It is interesting to note that both Generals Beg and Durrani were not seeking approval but were apprising the Prime Minister of an established practice. Similarly, Lieutenant General Fazle Haq, the then Governor of the North West Frontier Province of Pakistan (NWFP), whose links with the drug cartels as well as ISI officials were well known, played a seminal role in persuading some drug lords to provide weapons and other assistants to Sikh terrorists.

As regards the vehicle, the Indian experience reveals that terrorist groups in India regularly used narcotics smugglers who are familiar with the clandestine border crossing, as couriers for arms and explosives as well as money to finance terrorist attacks in India. In the present scenario, the main vehicle for ISI-supported narco-terrorism is the underworld syndicate controlled by Dawood Ibrahim and Co. (known as D Company). The liberalisation of gold imports and the tightening of Indian west coast security made a significant dent in D Company's business, compelling it to look for new avenues. D Company's rapid progress was ensured by its entrenched network in the Gulf– Arabian Sea–West Coast area, its shipping infrastructure, extensive international operations and knowledge of smuggling routes that facilitated the movement of contraband, *hawala* network and drug trade supported by the ISI, Pakistan Army, Taliban, Al Qaeda, JeM and other terrorist groups working from Pakistan. To facilitate this process, the syndicate had an extensive network of contacts and infrastructure located at strategic points, which caused Dawood to be listed as a global terrorist by the US. Subsequently, he was included on the UN sanction list as an associate of the Taliban and Al Qaeda.

Apart from other sources, published materials quoting Pakistani politicians and generals has brought out the links between the narcotics trade and intelligence agencies. The CIA report 'Heroin in Pakistan: Sowing the Wind' brings out the fact that Pakistan used drug money to finance the war in Afghanistan as well as terrorist activities in Punjab and Kashmir. The study by the CIA cited numerous reports which established irrefutably that the ISI, the Directorate of Military Intelligence in Pakistan and its field units have used drug money and continue to use to finance terrorism and secessionism in neighbouring India. According to an estimate, the heroin industry in Pakistan is worth over a billion rupees and the drug mafia in Pakistan, in connivance with the defence forces and ISI, has become a law in itself and the so-called democracy in Pakistan is only on paper. Muslim terrorist groups all over the world are financed through drug money being generated by the ISI. The fencing of the Indo-Pakistan border in Punjab and part of Rajasthan has considerably checked smuggling activities through these borders; consequently, the J&K border with Pakistan not being fenced is being exploited by drug smugglers in a major way and the main route runs through the Jammu and Kathua districts. The long coastline and porous land border of Gujarat and Pakistan, including the border district of Kutch, the Saurashtra region, particularly the Jamnagar and Junagadh districts, Banaskandha and Ahmedabad, are the main trafficking routes and centres of narcotics smuggling in Gujarat. The IB officers posted in these areas keep a close watch on all these activities and report to the government so as to enable to army and border security forces to take suitable actions, such as surgical strikes, from time to time.

NINE

BIOLOGICAL SABOTAGE: THE CHINESE THREAT AND BIOTERRORISM

'A ruler could use any methods and means to attain the expected goals.'

The origin and history of biological warfare can be dated to the fourth century BC. Kautilya's *Arthashastra* (Book XIV) touches on one aspect of chemical and biological warfare, stating that smoke coming from a burning powder made out of the skin and excretions of certain reptiles, animals and birds could cause mass madness and blindness among the enemy.

He goes on to suggest the doctrine of a silent war, of a war of assassinations against enemies and his approval of secret agents who could kill enemy kings in order to create confusion and panic among the enemy army.

The biblical story of the Exodus mentions ten plagues that God inflicted on the Egyptians for the pharaoh to free the Jews from slavery: blood, frogs, vermin, flies, murrain, boils, hail, locusts, death of their firstborns. The idea was to use all available means to hit them where it hurt the most, to influence the ministerial consensus and the royal edict. 'Biological assaults' can be a powerful instrument to influence the enemy's decisions and to drive home your point.

Biological warfare can be defined as the use of bacteria, viruses and fungi to kill or harm the target. An example of biological warfare is weaponized anthrax.

One of the very first examples of biological warfare is the poisoning of wells and water supplies of settlements. Among the earliest to do this were the Assyrians, who poisoned enemy waters with fungus during the sixth century BC, hitting right at the biggest lifeline for any civilisation and thereby rendering the enemy delirious and unable to fight.

One of the most talked-about pandemics in history is the Black Death, which some people believe was a biological attack by the Mongol warriors of the Golden Horde. The Black Death, which swept through Europe, the Near East, and North Africa in the middle of the 14th century, was probably the greatest public health disaster in recorded history and one of the most dramatic examples ever of the emergence of a new lethal disease. The Black Death is said to have originated in the east and moved through China and central Asia to knock on the doors of Europe. What is of interest is that along with the advent of the disease, another force was relentlessly advancing towards Europe: the Mongolian hordes. Their paths are uncannily synched, which is what leads to theories of there having been a connection between the two. Crimea, present-day Ukraine, as the entry point to Europe for the Mongols, surely played a pivotal role as the proximal source from which the Mediterranean basin was infected. According to the recordings of 14th-century historians, while besieging the Crimean city of Caffa, the army grew ill with the plague themselves. What do they do? They decide to use the disease plaguing them to their advantage and they, very clinically, pass it forward.

It is mentioned in Italian memoirs of that period that the Mongols, petrified by the diseases that had killed thousands of them, and as a last attempt to enter the city walls that lay in front of them, catapulted the rotting corpses of their warriors who had died of the plague into the city. Understandably, the city didn't fare too well against that. Soon, the piles of rotting corpses tainted the air and poisoned the water supply.

Many from Caffa tried to sail to Genoa or Venice in an attempt to escape and carried with them the pestilential disease into Europe. Some people blame this for the spread of the bubonic plague into Europe. And it wasn't just the Mongols who turned to such fiendish methods for colonial expansion; some people say that the British, in the 16th century, had used smallpox against the native Americans in America. The natives had not previously been exposed to the 'white man's diseases. And the spreading of the white men's diseases among the natives possibly wasn't just an unfortunate coincidence either. The British would give gifts of smallpox-infected items like blankets to the villagers. These infected the non-resistant natives, wiping out villages. This was sanctioned by the crown and the government, with an intent to kill. This was one of the first widespread use of biological warfare.

After this, the use of biological warfare made a reappearance in the early 1900s. The early cases of biological sabotage followed a 'pay it forward' policy: in most cases, an ailment that was already inflicting a foreign invader was passed on to the invaded nation unknowingly or on purpose by the invaders, with the aim of levelling the playing field a little. The motivation in such cases, and these motivations can even occur today, was the fear of losing the competitive or strategic advantage owing to a plague ailing a nation, and hence the nation decides to cause its competitors to contract the same ailment as well.

The advances in germ theory, the new knowledge that diseases were caused by microorganisms and bacteriology in general brought forth more sophisticated methods of weaponizing the diseases and would later go on to even custom-create diseases.

Biological sabotage, a new form of biological warfare, was undertaken by Germany during WWI. Anthrax and glanders first appear on the scene. In 1925, the Geneva Protocol banned the use of gases and bacteriological methods in warfare; the pact was signed by 140 parties.

With the start of WWII, many countries started researching, mass producing and stockpiling biological weaponry.

To reiterate, it wasn't just the Axis of evil, i.e., the Axis powers led by Germany, but even Britain and the rest of the allied Europe who were involved in the proliferation of biological weapons technology back then. Soon, a number of pathogens were weaponised effectively, including anthrax, brucellosis and botulism.

The Scottish island of Gruinard, which was quarantined for 56 years after extensive anthrax tests, still stands testimony to just how dangerous and long-lasting the impacts are.

The British programme was the first to successfully weaponize a variety of pathogens and to produce them at an industrial scale, although Britain never used these weapons. When the US joined the war, the British mounted pressure for the creation of a similar program for an Allied pooling of resources. Before long, the US had facilities for the mass production of anthrax, brucellosis and botulism. Thankfully, the war ended before any of these could really be put to any sinister use against civilians.

The Japanese ran the most notorious programme at the time. Their Army Unit 731, run by Lieutenant General Shiro Ishii, became a term eerily synonymous with 'biological annihilation' to the Allies. Under the sanction of Imperial Japan, Unit 731 conducted its research on human subjects, which often ended in fatality. Although the research lacked the technical edge of similar research being undertaken elsewhere, it made up for it, by sheer indiscriminate brutality and uninhibited human experimentation. Their Manchurian campaign saw brutal use of these weapons on Chinese soldiers and civilians alike.

In the 1940s, the Japanese air force bombed the Chinese sub-province of Ningbo with ceramic bombs filled with fleas carrying the bubonic plague. This delivery allegedly resulted in the death of around 400,000 people. During the Zhejiang-Jiangxi campaign in 1942, around 100,000 Japanese soldiers fell ill, and many lost their lives in a biological attack.

The 1950s saw the weaponization of the plague, tularaemia and later equine encephalomyelitis and vaccinia viruses. In 1969, at the height of the Cold War, the UK and the Warsaw Pact separately introduced proposals to ban all biological weapons. In 1972, the Biological and Toxic Weapons Convention was signed by the UK, US and USSR, among other nations, thus banning the stockpiling of these weapons except for protective and peaceful research.

The effectiveness of these treaties was questioned by Ken Alibeck in his book *Biohazard*, in which he disclosed the activities that still went on in the Soviet biological warfare industry well into the 1990s.

A more credible and convincing statement came from Alexander Couzminov in his book *Biological Espionage* (London, Greenhill Books, 2005). Couzminov has excellent scientific credentials and was recruited by the Soviet foreign intelligence service in 1980 and served there till 1992. His Ph.D. in molecular biophysics and his long span of service with the Soviet secret agency made his work a reference book for all spies dealing with biological weaponry. Couzminov's main tasks included biological espionage, acquiring open-source information from foreign academia and industry, placing and preparation for biological terrorism and sabotage and assisting the biological weapons programme. His job also involved placing spies into sensitive biotechnology positions in the West and sending information and specimens collected from these spies back to Moscow.

In the last century, modern biology has produced nearly miraculous cures from such intractable diseases of human beings. But to the surprise of many security analysts, the same scientists have explored its practicability for biological warfare. Unlike chemical and nuclear arms, these other weapons of mass destruction, the biological agents, are living. This makes their reach many times greater than the range of nuclear or chemical destruction. Life thrives on, and life finds a way, and mostly so with microorganisms. Being a living weapon, it can spread and cause impacts for years, taking swathes of land under its influence. And it penetrates into all civilian walks of life, not just the military, obliterating national security apparatuses, and decimating health workers and policymakers and just about anyone in its path. What's more? Being stealthy and unstoppable is just the beginning. It can even adapt, evolve and mutate with newer strains. This makes it the ultimate self-upgrading weaponry, that uses nature's intelligence to learn and adapt, at the back of any counter measures employed by its target.

From the beginning of the twenty-first century, a new disruption to the world order has been in the offing. As the new world-leader-in-waiting, China is desperate to be seen as the new strong kid on the block. And thus, as it happened in the case of Germany and later the Soviet Union, the ensuing atmosphere of competition and distrust almost guarantees that belligerent countries waver from their earlier peacetime resolves and foray into the forbidden.

In this context, the relevance of Chinese biological weaponry came to the limelight in 2020, when a Chinese research fellow was intercepted and taken into custody at Logan Airport by the FBI, when he was trying to board a flight to China. It was found that he had in his procession a few vials of smuggled biological material. He was later found to be a research fellow at the renowned Harvard University in Boston in the US. According to the FBI, one more researcher who was actually a Chinese army officer was also arrested along with the Chinese research fellow at the airport. Much more valuable and sensational information is expected from further interrogation of the arrested. All this resembles an international spy novel of Stephen Coonts in real life!

Further to this came the news of the arrest of Dr. Charles Lieber, Harvard University's Head of Department of Chemistry and Chemical Biology, for not disclosing to the Department of Defence secret monthly payments of $50,000 from China and the receipt of millions of dollars more to help set up a chemical/biological research laboratory in China.

This may or may not have had a connection with the pandemic, but it underlines China's rising interest in bio-chemical experimentation using international scholars and the secretive manner in which this was undertaken, and remunerations were made raises suspicions.

China is believed to have an advanced chemical warfare programme that includes research, development, production and weaponisation. It is also said that China has a wide variety of delivery systems for chemical agents, which include artillery, rockets, aerial bombs, ballistic missiles and sprayers. There are reasons to believe that, despite being a signatory to the Chemical Weapons Convention (CWC) on December 30, 1996, China possesses an advanced biotechnology infrastructure to produce weaponised biological agents, though it has constantly refuted this claim.

Pursuant to the Chemical and Biological Weapons Control and Warfare Elimination Act of 1991 (BWCWEA), the US government-imposed trade sanctions on five Chinese individuals, two Chinese companies and one Hong Kong company for knowingly and materially contributing to Iran's chemical weapons programme.

In this light, the emergence of the Covid-19 coronavirus in early 2020 has yet to be assessed with all available information. Coronaviruses, with DNA/genetic engineering, can be an offensive biological warfare weapon, say researchers.

Private Chinese companies have long been accused of close links with Chinese defence establishments, indicating a dual use of technology made for civilian purposes. The outbreak of the Covid-19 coronavirus in December 2019 points fingers at a Chinese civil-military coupling in the bioengineering and medical fields. In July 2019, in a rare incident, a few Chinese scientists and researchers were accused of spying and hence stripped of their access to Canada's National Microbiology Lab.

Americans and some other western countries suspected that the virus striking Wuhan in China may have a connection to Wuhan being home to two laboratories linked to China's bio-warfare programme. According to Israeli warfare experts, the strains that went on to cause the epidemic might have originated in a Wuhan laboratory.

Since 1952, China has professed to recognise itself as legally bound to the Geneva Protocol, which prohibits the use of biological and chemical weapons. Besides, China is party to the major international agreements regulating biological weapons, having acceded to the Biological and Toxin Weapons Convention (BTWC).

India has ratified the Biological Weapons Convention (BWC) and pledges to abide by its obligations. There is no clear evidence, either circumstantial or otherwise, that India ever produced any offensive biological weapon. India does possess the scientific capability and infrastructure to launch such a programme.

However, former Defence Minister Manohar Parikar asserted that India should have an effective system to 'prevent' potential consequences from the use of chemical and biological weapons in the wake of the changing threat perception and security concerns. He was referring to the reported use of chemical weapons in Afghanistan, which is close to the Indian subcontinent. Echoing the ex-Defence Minister's concern, the Chief of Indian Army then said that the armed forces must be prepared for all kinds of threats as such weapons could be used by an adversary.

The various reports alluding to the existence of a formidable Chinese chemical and biological weapons arsenal should concern India, primarily due to the known nexus and technology sharing between China and Pakistan. China itself has a shared boundary with India, and its proximity and common border only help the delivery systems for biological agents.

India has a well-developed biological infrastructure for pharmaceutical production. However, the late APJ Abdul Kalam, while he was president of India, asserted that 'India will not produce biological weapons. ' The nation's moral ethics and the collective conscience of the citizens, all forbid our governments to venture into the development of something as immoral as biological weapons. But this does not mean that the nation should remain oblivious to the strides being made elsewhere with weaponized biological agents.

The coronavirus pandemic and intelligence failures

The Covid-19 pandemic, the coronavirus, and nations failing to halt its uninhibited march across the globe surely have glaring indications of intelligence failure on the part of every world government. There were failures in detecting the clandestine creation of the virus (if that was in fact how it originated) and in seeing through the misinformation China spread initially on the severity of the pandemic. All the probes US intelligence had planted for intelligence gathering in China proved ineffective in determining the exact count of casualties in China, and this misrepresented the gravity of the situation and greatly impeded the US response preparation to the advancing pandemic.

The major challenge that the medical community and the nations' administrations faced in this pandemic were the many unknowns about it. The pandemic happened in an era of data and information, but, ironically, the nations found themselves in almost as much darkness about the pandemic as the Europeans were when hit by the bubonic plague in the 14th century.

The plague had swept across central Asia and entered Europe through Crimea, although the records don't show as much devastation in Asia as in Europe. The Chinese, Indians, Persians, Armenians, Georgians, Mesopotamians, Ethiopians, Turks, Egyptians and Arabs all seem to have been struck first by the advancing plague, but they all seemed to have knocked it off comparatively earlier. Did the eastern countries find a way to deal with it? Had they discovered a cure or a precaution that could halt the spread? It took Europe more than six years and millions of casualties before they could link its spread to house rats. The earlier theories of the disease vector being 'miasma', or the noxious air emanating from rotting organic matter kept the medical personnel misguided and confused for decades while millions perished–all owing to the delay in linking the spread to rats.

Sharing valuable information, broadcasting directives, the mass media, and a well-connected global network that could send out early warning signs of an onset: none of these existed during the bubonic plague. All of them exist today. Then why did we find ourselves as helpless and disconnected today when confronting the COVID-19 challenge? Why hasn't the information era helped in getting the right information at the right time? The answer is down to deliberate blocking of information or even the spreading of false narratives by countries when instead, they should have elevated themselves beyond their infighting and competitiveness.

Maybe China didn't quite gauge just how out-of-hand things would get when it was trying to save face before its own people and its reputation before the world. The country that already boasts of having dethroned the West as the leader of the new world order and keeps its citizen feeding off from the nationalist pride it condones and encourages, understandably tried all it could to downplay the gravitas of the situation, to hide its incompetence in the face of the virus outbreak. This obviously proved to be catastrophic.

Such blocking of potentially lifesaving information, especially regarding a common enemy, by countries to hide their own failures and to avoid a global reputational loss has in itself become a whole new threat to the world in general. The threat of withholding critical information in an information-dependant age.

It is ridiculous to even think of such deliberations and ploys, on the part of world nations, especially when confronted with something that threatens the very human race. But it did happen. We can't be sure at this point what is the truth behind the origination and the onset of the pandemic, but it is surely one of the scenarios below.

One of the hypotheses below is most likely to be very close to the truth:

Hypothesis 1: China loses patience in its wait to realize Xi Jinping's 'China Dream'. It can no longer suppress its ambition to be regarded for the wonder it believes it is. Its ambitions now overrun its sense and sensibility. It creates a weaponized SARS strain and releases it to the world with the motive of initiating the disruption that it had been waiting for. Consequently, the world economy is shattered while China emerges as the new economic behemoth. Global stocks plummet. Chinese corporations take the cue and step forth to drastically increase ownership in strained international companies in the guise of angel investors. China ends up with majority stakes in global corporations and attains economic pre-eminence. In the process of spreading the pandemic, it kills a few of its own first, to conceal the act of espionage, but the communist regime feels that the prize at the end will be worth it.

And all this is not just to achieve economic hegemony; China wishes to cause a complete upheaval in the world's perception of itself, and more importantly, that of the US. It understands that global orders have a tendency to shift quickly. After all, a botched intervention in the Suez Canal conflict was all that it took to bare the vulnerabilities of British power and mark the end of UK's reign as a global leader in people's minds.

With the coronavirus, China expects to create a Suez-like embarrassment, but for the US—to strip the US of its aura and expose its unsuitability to continue as the world's leader; to depict it as a burnt out and distracted regime whose failings herald the need for a different vision. And it seems to be going China's way, too. Miscalculations (fed by China's misrepresentation of critical data), by all key institutions, from the White House and the Department of Homeland Security to the Centre for Disease Control and Prevention (CDC), have shaken the world's confidence in the capacity and competence of US governance. Perhaps towards the later part of the calamity, once the goals have been achieved, Chinese pharmaceutical giants might bring out of nowhere, the vaccine or the antidote, thus applying the handbrake when most convenient for Beijing.

Hypothesis 2: The Hong Kong protests might have been what set things into motion. The subversive soft power and mass-media propaganda that the US is capable of have been intimidating China for a long time and probably the Hong Kong protest flared by US-sponsored NGOs just might have pushed China over the edge. China desperately seeks to tame the protesting populace who now seem to be going out of control. It cannot tolerate a Hong Kong Spring and decides to quell free thought, even if it means stupefying the leaders of the protest. Whatever the motivation, it accelerates its SARS biological research program. The coronavirus thus created inadvertently escapes the laboratory containment, thus becoming China's Frankenstein monster. Chinese leadership goes into a frenzy about how to explain this to the world. It feels its ambitions will be bared and fears a backlash. Hence it decides to conceal the truth and introduces the virus to the world as a naturally formed SARS strain and hides its genetically engineered origins, in other words, the fact that it is a supervirus. The world now has been given misguiding intelligence, which has been extremely detrimental to the success of the nations' response strategies. Obviously,

China was far more successful since it had known from the beginning what it was dealing with.

Hypothesis 3: There is no foul play in the origin of the virus, SARS self-mutates into newer strains naturally and finds its way to humans, but China finds itself unprepared to counter the outbreak. Millions of lives are probably lost but China closes down the impacted provinces and manipulates the data coming out, thereby heavily understating its casualty count, in an effort to save the pride of the communist regime.

The truth might very well be any of the three hypotheses above. It can be the least sinister looking Hypothesis 3, but that doesn't mean any future possibility of Hypotheses 1 and 2 need not be studied by intelligence agencies of the world. The virus that swept across the world starting January 2020, caused unprecedented threats to national and international security, rather than being just a public health emergency. Many world leaders unanimously opined that the aftermath would resemble that of a major war involving a large number of casualties. Intelligence services will have a major role in this struggle in keeping their respective countries safe during the spread of the pandemic. They will largely play in the shadows, keeping in view the basic principles of spying. Many are of the view that the Covid-19 is the worst intelligence failure in human history.

There are many ways that intelligence agencies, including the IB, could contribute to fighting this war against the deadly virus. The CIA reportedly has a dedicated facility now known as the National Center for Medical Intelligence (NCMI) to fight Covid-19, as a clearing agency for the US about the virus. It will provide policy makers assessments about the impact of the virus while its parent body will look into the national, international, political, economic, and social impact, besides suggesting means and methods to counter the disease. According to media reports, in January-February 2020, US intelligence services warned the Trump administration about the worldwide threat of the coronavirus spreading from China and becoming a pandemic, but the president allegedly either dismissed or ignored the warnings. In this way it was not as much an intelligence failure as a policy failure.

Another way for an intelligence agency to counter the coronavirus is to collect information that others want to keep a secret through stealing or spying. The intelligence community will be able to provide policymakers valuable information unavailable from normal sources about foreign and internal anti-government agents. US agencies have reported that China concealed the spread of the virus initially and Russia came out with draconian lockouts at a later stage. So, spies in India, the US and its allies could come out with verifying information on its actual origin, its spread and its impact. This intelligence could come from espionage, including century old agent-running and modern technical gadgets.

The third way that intelligence agencies could respond to the virus and future pandemics is by countering misinformation. Both the US and China are now engaged in a propaganda battle as to who is leading the world in defeating the virus and whether democratic or authoritarian governments can better protect citizens, in order to discredit each other. The Chinese regime is promoting a conspiracy theory that the US military was instrumental in importing the new epidemic to China. Some people in the US, on the other hand, suggest that China deliberately invented the virus as a biological weapon. During the Cold War period, the US government successfully formulated a strategy to counter KGB misinformation about HIV. As a result of this, in 1987, Moscow had to abruptly disown the HIV conspiracy theory. The same strategy could be used even now to counter Covid-19 misinformation.

Bioterrorism

Bioterrorism is the deliberate human act of disease vectoring and proliferation of viruses, bacteria, or other germs by terrorist or extremist elements. The pathogens thus spread can be naturally occurring, or biologically enhanced and are usually aimed at a creating an unstoppable contagion in a target populace, with the intent to cause fatality or incapacity in people, livestock or crops. The terrorists could themselves obtain the vials or germ agents by stealing then from a lab or could be working as proxies on behalf of a hostile nation and could provide the needed weaponised germs engineered in the target country's own labs.

Biological attacks can prove much more devastating for a target nation than hundreds of sparsely planted bombs. This is a self-upgrading weapon, assisted by nature and life itself, in the face of any counterattack or attempt at neutralisation by the target. It could make itself immune to available antibiotics and vaccines, thanks to the genetic enhancements received in a bio lab and later by self-mutations.

According to the CDC, *Bacillus anthracis*, the bacteria that causes anthrax, is one of the most likely agents to be used in a biological attack. Per the CDC, weaponised anthrax appeals to bioterrorists for the following reasons:

- Anthrax spores are easily found in nature, can be produced in a lab, and can last for a long time in the environment.

- Anthrax makes a good weapon because it can be released quietly and without anyone knowing. The microscopic spores could be put into powders, sprays, food and water. Because they are so small, you may not be able to see, smell, or taste them.

India can imagine how vulnerable it is to such a threat, owing to the mass impact it can have and the ease with which terrorists can procure such weapons, not to mention the help they can always seek from our neighbours, one of whom has already made a name for itself for having possible shady and extremely sinister biological labs. Vials of pathogens can be routed via different countries, as is done with Chinese arms coming into India. In fact, an upswing in technology proliferation and black markets for biological weapons, too, cannot be written off after the dust settles on the pandemic.

TEN

NAXALISM: ARMED REBELLION AGAINST THE GOVERNMENT AND DEMOCRACY

According to the Ministry of Home Affairs of the Government of India, during 2019, there were 117 attacks by Naxalites, which killed 311 people. Naxalites are reportedly the deadliest extremist organisation in India and the CPI (Maoist) stands sixth among the world's terrorist organisations. According to the US State Department, nearly 26 percent of the extremist attacks in India are carried out by the CPI (Maoist). The other dangerous terrorist and/or extremist organisations are the Taliban, the ISI, Al Shabab in Africa, Boko Haram in Africa and the Communist party of the Philippines. US documents further say that India stands fourth among countries that face terrorist threats. The top three countries are Afghanistan, Syria and Iraq. During the year 2018, India faced terrorist attacks in 29 states and 971 people were killed. Out of these attacks, 67 percent were in Jammu and Kashmir. CPI (Maoist) areas in the state of

Chhattisgarh stood in the second position in the proportion of terrorist attacks.

An early 2019 directive from the United Command of Security and intelligence agencies at the centre was to shoot at sight at Maoists, in the wake of a maiden incident where drones or unmanned aerial vehicles (UAVs) were seen hovering over a strategically important CRPF camp in the worst Naxal-violence-affected district of Sukma in the Chhattisgarh Bustar region in November 2019. Small drones emitting red and white light were seen flying near the CRPF camp in Kistaram and Pallodi for two to three days in October 2019. The drones emitted a low whistling sound that drew the attention of the camp guards. The troops assumed an offensive position and sounded an alert across all nearby camps that possible trouble by Naxals was anticipated.

This incident rang alarm bells in the security establishment, leading intelligence agencies to a dealer in Mumbai who was suspected of having sold the drones to some unidentified Naxal cadres. Agencies were particularly concerned as the two camps where the drones were spotted are located deep inside the Naxal hotbed, do not have proper road connectivity and have witnessed regular movements of armed Maoist cadres as the area shares borders with Odisha and Maharashtra and leads to the jungle corridor of Andhra Pradesh. Despite all the efforts taken by the Centre and respective state governments to curtail the Naxal menace, Naxalites continue to flourish. This is undoubtedly a matter that poses a security threat to the whole country.

Left-wing extremism (LWE)

Left-wing extremism could be defined as groups working for change in the social system who come to power through violence, which they call the people's armed revolution. It denounces peaceful established political processes. LWE politics supports social equality and egalitarianism, opposing social hierarchy. The political terms 'left' and 'right' go back to the French Revolution (1789-99), referring to the seating arrangements of those opposing and supporting the monarchy. Those who sat on the left side of the French National Assembly opposed the monarchy and supported revolution and those seated on the right supported the traditional institution of the monarchy. In the late nineteenth century, 'left-wing' was applied to those who were un-orthodox in their political and social views.

Left-wing extremists, commonly known as Naxalites in India, were formed in 1969 in Calcutta. Some LWE leaders sneaked into China and were said to have met Mao Tse Tung and sought his support for unleashing a similar revolution in India. Mao asked for a map of India and advised his LWE leaders to locate a safe place bordering other countries in order to withdraw and hide after every guerrilla attack. It is believed that it was Mao who taught guerrilla warfare to Indian left-wing extremists. To achieve their final goal of revolution, Mao himself pointed out a place named Naxalbari bordering West Bengal and Nepal. This was how the word 'Naxalites' came into existence.

In the age-old social and economic systems prevailing in the rural areas of India, namely Zamindarism, casteism and religious discrimination, land was owned by a group of so-called upper castes. The marginal farmers, poor agricultural workers, tribals and 'lower caste' people have been forced to work in the agriculture field and produce products for the *zamindars, bhoomikars* and other upper castes. These forced labourers were never allowed to question their masters and were forced to live in poverty from generation to generation at the whims and fancies of their masters. The British rulers did nothing substantial to free the poor peasants and workers from the bondage of the affluent for obvious reasons. Even after Independence, the succeeding governments both at the Centre as well as in the states did not pay much attention to the uplift of the poor. This situation paved the way for the LWE to brainwash poor villagers and get their support, luring them in the hope of relief from bondage and distribution of land among them. Though the aim of LWE looks outwardly genuine, in reality their actions of violence and theory of annihilation of the rich were not acceptable to a democratic government. As a result of this, the government started deploying the police force and CRPF to counter LWE attacks.

The LWE were later divided into splinter groups, following ideological differences and personality cults among the leaders. Some of these splinter groups are the CPI (Marxists-Leninists), People's War Group (PWG), the CPI (Janasakti) and Maoist Communist Centre (MCC). The origin of left-wing extremism can be traced to when the Communist Party of India - Marxist split in 1967, when some ultra-revolutionary leaders left and formed the CPI (ML) in the theory of armed revolution. These LWE groups established their presence in nearly 28 states of India, including strongholds such as Chhattisgarh, Andhra Pradesh, Maharashtra, Madhya Pradesh, Bihar, Orissa and present-day Jharkhand. They concentrate in the jungles and try to wield the support of local tribes through small finances support, indoctrination, threats and coercion.

According to the Ministry of Home Affairs (MHA), more than 180 districts have been affected, mainly the border districts of Madhya Pradesh, Andhra Pradesh, Maharashtra, Jharkhand and Bihar. Naxalite insurgency is an ongoing menace and threat to the national security resulting in regular encounters between the LWE cadres and the police force. Hundreds of people, including police personnel, have been killed every year since 2005. Naxalite groups are aware of the fact that in order to sustain their activities, they require sophisticated, modern weaponry. To procure these weapons, they need a huge amount of money.

There are reports that these groups collect huge amounts as protection money, estimated to be Rs. 4 or 5 crore per annum for allowing the collection of *tendu* leaves for making *beedis*, cigarettes and other tobacco products. Besides, the Naxalites receive another Rs 5 to 10 crore per year from paper mill owners as a price to ensure the smooth cutting of bamboo from the forests.

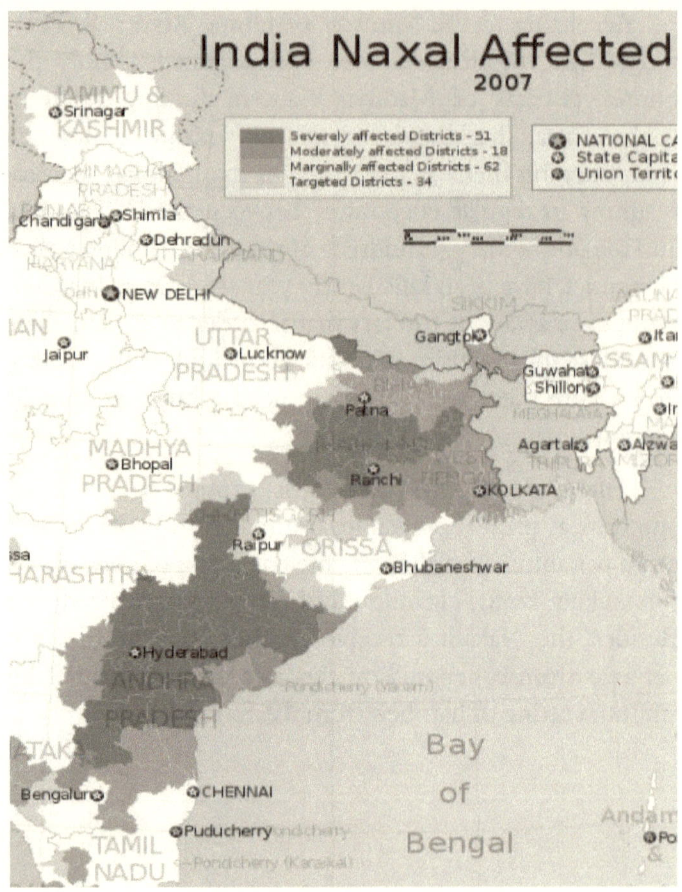

source: Wikipedia

They frequently target tribal villagers, police personnel and government employees in what they say is a fight for land rights and jobs for the poor and marginalised. They claim that they follow a strategy of rural revolution similar to the protracted people's war against the government and present establishment.

The crossbreeding and interrelationship of Maoist groups with militant organisations, Northeast insurgents and radical Islamic organisations, particularly for the logistics of terror, continue to be a key concern for the internal security of India. At the same time, many factors imply that China has a role in encouraging left-wing extremism in India. The CPI (Maoist) being a member of the Coordination Committee of Maoist Parties and Organisations of South Asia (CCOMPOSA), has the blessing of the Communist Party of China (CPC).

There is a flourishing smugglers market in China for small arms, very likely with the knowledge of the state. Naxalite weapons procurement usually takes the Nepal, Myanmar and Bangladesh routes, but it is difficult to conceive that there isn't funding or material provided directly from China. After all, Maoists do belong to the ultra-left brotherhood of Chinese communism, along with Maoist comrades in Nepal (Communist Party of Nepal Maoists), Sri Lanka (Ceylon Communist Party Maoist) as well as a Bangladesh (Purba Banglar Communist Party–ML). The recoveries of Chinese-made arms and radio sets from the Naxals is a substantial indication of continuing Maoist-China linkages.

Anti-Naxalite operations

The first deaths from combat with Naxal insurgency began in 1980. In 2009 alone, around 1100 people were reported to have been killed, including 600 civilians, 300 security personnel and 200 Naxalites. In order to counter the LWE atrocities, various states started deploying special task forces for anti-Naxal operations. But most of these personnel led by middle-level officers posted in Naxal areas consider it a punishment posting and hence lack interest. From 1996 to 2018, there were a total of 14,369 deaths, including 3440 security personnel, 4041 Naxalites and 8051 civilians.

In 2019, the government of India and affected state governments took special measures to deal with Naxalism, which was judged to be the biggest internal security threat for these states. A greater budget allocation was earmarked for Anti-Naxal operations, including for the procurement of the latest weapons and modern training for security personnel. More money is being pumped into the rural areas exclusively for the social and economic uplift of the poor masses.

The MHA claimed, 'Naxalism has been buried twenty feet under the ground'. Incidences of violence and deaths were considerably reduced during 2019-2020. During the period 2017-2020, nearly Rs 3000 crore have been allotted under special central assistance to contain Naxalism and connected activities in affected areas.

Intelligence and other security agencies have perhaps the most important role to play in countering LWE terrorism. The IB closely monitors them and reports to the government almost on a daily basis, as these extremist elements can very quickly regain potency and disrupt the social fabric. A separate division was created as early as 2006 in the Home ministry to coordinate and collate the inputs from intelligence agencies and accordingly give instructions to the state machinery. It also coordinates the implementation of various developmental schemes launched in the affected districts and ensures proper utilisation of funds to each state.

Lack of communication and transportation facilities and basic necessities for villagers and tribes and the overall backwardness of the Naxal-affected areas are indeed the main reasons why Naxalites get the support of poor locals to pursue the philosophy of armed revolution to overthrow democratically elected governments. The poor and marginalised sections of the tribal area are always bearing the brunt of LWE.

Surprisingly, some liberal intellectuals fall prey to the Maoist philosophy and propaganda without knowing the hidden agenda of these extremist elements. These intellectuals support the LWE either out of ignorance or deliberately to get prominence and the attention of the media. The IB has unearthed some incidents in which these so-called intellectuals received foreign support, including money from like-minded anti-establishment NGOs and movements and anti-Indian individuals. (For security reasons, the details of these cannot be published.) It is a fact that some youth have a romantic illusion about LWE and are attracted to the ideology of Naxalism. The presence of women cadres in the LWE outfits further attracts the youth.

Some of the important actions of the special anti-Naxalite division in the MHA, are:

1. Building the capability of states to combat LWE

2. Deployment of CRPF and central paramilitary forces in highly sensitive areas

3. Regular reviews of the security scenario and threat perception

4. More financial aid for strengthening infrastructure, equipment, modern weaponry, vehicles, etc.

5. Acquisition of sniper rifles and drones by Naxalites is a matter of concern for the security forces. The Government of India approved a scheme for the modernisation of police forces in 2017, with additional perks for those personnel deployed in affected. (It may be added that Maoists presently use the most sophisticated and up-to-date weaponry procured from terrorist groups abroad. Money launderers and arms smugglers are also reportedly helping the Naxalites in procuring these weapons.)

ELEVEN

REBELLION AGAINST GOVERNMENT AND DEMOCRACY: THE LOOMING THREAT OF THE NON-STATE ACTORS

This chapter deals with the issue of non-state, quasi-actors and the existence of anarchical self-rule tranches between the elected governments and the people. Through the first decade of the twenty-first century we saw governments across the Middle East and South Asia increasingly losing power to **Armed Non-State Actors (or ANSAs)** as they inserted themselves at a mezzanine level of rule between the government and the people.

Although at first this may sound like an idea conceivable only in the ungoverned terrains of Afghanistan, or in a post-war, unsupervised Iraq, it would be extremely shortsighted to think that this cannot happen anywhere. It can happen in developed countries as well, where it can exist in small pockets.

Local populations often regard such ANSAs as espousing their religious, ethnic or social causes.

Communities that feel marginalized tend to look at them for protection and sustenance. On the exterior they look messianic to the weaker sections of society, providing them vital services, but in reality, these actors encourage dissociation and state fragmentation. In their efforts to squeeze themselves into a mezzanine layer between the elected government and its people, they undermine effective governance and development.

And they have been successful, too, in many parts of the globe. Many ANSA rulers enjoy a wide range of formal statuses, and some even have a stabilizing influence at home and regionally.

In the Kurdish region in Iraq, ANSAs have been granted some autonomy by the state's federal structure, thereby granting them power to govern.

In Gaza or Somaliland, they are not formally independent, but they operate as near-state entities, being in a suspended state for state recognition. They have acquired land and converted it into autonomous regions, into self-declared states, albeit without international recognition. By doing so, they have transfigured themselves from militant groups into governments, even democratically elected through elections conducted within their realms.

Many of these quasi-states continue to legitimize themselves by increasingly gaining informal recognitions from foreign governments, who sent delegations to them or open trade offices in their territories, all of which invariably irks the host nation's government. ANSAs usually benefit from proving the longevity and stability of their regime, or their usability for proxy wars against the host government on the behest of a foreign government, since all that ushers in legitimacy approvals and recognition.

Sometimes the ANSAs are inbred by the host state. In such cases the activities of the non-state actors bleed outside of the state borders, especially into neighboring democracies where the host state intends to cause destabilisation and fragmentation.

By seeking to embed themselves irrevocably in a country's political system and win exclusive control over a segment of the population, ANSAs jeopardise domestic stability.

ANSAs with origins in say, Pakistan, but with their fraternity's increasing impression on Indian soil is a matter requiring extreme attention and watchfulness by the nation's intelligence.

Disenfranchised local communities often identify with non-state actors, thanks to a shared religious affiliation, ethnicity, or frustration towards the ruling government. Seeing no advantage in looking to the state for help, they see these mezzanine groups as kindred, articulating their grievances and seeking to address them. Drawing on their welfare support organisations and militias, ANSAs can build public devotion and self-durability in a way that governments find difficult to do. Many of these ANSAs even use their external cashflows to supply education, welfare, and emergency aid to its supporters. All these being fruitful investments in return for the devotion of its subjects, its people.

Deep roots in local communities and an organized style of functioning are the marks of the most successful ANSAs.

By fusing together religious studies with social welfare projects and political indulgences and adding to all that an occasional rejection of the primacy of ruling regime and sometimes even violent displays of strength, ANSAs project themselves as layered and diversely assorted institutions.

The movement is a religious organisation, a cause-driven NGO, a political party, and a paramilitary force all at the same time. This makes it difficult for governments to isolate their criminal arms and selectively dismantle them.

Hezbollah of Lebanon, for example became a well-established political player domestically and regionally. Its success is attributed to it being multifaceted. Its political wing, 'Loyalty to the Resistance Bloc party' has representation in the Lebanese parliament, even when it didn't have any constitutional standing, even when it is considered a militant organisation by 18 countries, including the US and the EU.

Its influence increased after the 2008 Lebanese protests, when Hezbollah and its allies obtained eleven of the thirty cabinets seats, giving them veto power in the newly formed national unity government. It even had the new cabinet approve the draft policy statement that recognised Hezbollah and guaranteed it the right to even "liberate or recover occupied lands". It has in this respect become a kind of model organisation for many similar movements in the region, to a great extent replacing the Sunni Muslim brotherhood.

It has always enjoyed mentorship from the Shia Iran, in that it acts as Iran's proxy in the Iran-Israel conflict. The Hezbollah dominates southern Lebanon and parts of Beirut and is fully developed with strong financial inflows, a military as well as an intelligence wing. Its churned out charismatic leaders like Hassan Nasrallah and has proven to have the military capability to take on one of the most militarily advanced nations in the world, during the Israel war in 2006. U.S. Secretary of Defense Robert Gates noted in April 2010 that the Hezbollah had more missiles and rockets than most governments.

All in all, this is yet another shadow war, the prize being the allegiance on the ground, where the nation's establishment has to work hard to counter the external creed's appeal to local populace.

In addition to all these points, the ISIS was an idea of a whole new boundless caliphate for implementing Sharia law. It was looked upon by millions as a proclamation of God's own state on earth. The issue with ideas is that they cannot be limited by geographical boundaries. Before the world took any serious notice, the 'idea of the Islamic State' had spread through vast swathes of the Middle East to the different ends of the world. As a Caliphate, it claimed religious, political, and military authority over all Muslims worldwide. Islamic clerics were drawn to it like moths drawn to fire, and in many places, the idea conceived was to establish little Islamic states in their own locales, Sharia being the only God-willed law of the land.

As recently as 2019, Reuters published an article in which it reported ISIS claiming that it has established its first "province" in India. Ridiculous as the claim comes across, let's delve a little into the influence ISIS has had and continues to have in India.

As per the report, ISIS called the area, located within India's northern state of Jammu and Kashmir, "Wilayah of Hind," or Hind province. It also claimed to have inflicted casualties upon Indian forces in a recent clash in Amshipora, a town in that state.

These claims by them "sought to emphasise the international nature of the struggle" following the group losing its self-styled "caliphate" in Iraq and Syria, wrote Nicolas Hénin, a former ISIS hostage and author of *Jihad Academy: The Rise of Islamic State,* in the Guardian.

ISIS likely sees Jammu and Kashmir, with its long-simmering Muslim-Hindu tensions, as promising territory.

Rita Katz, director of the SITE Intelligence Group, weighed in on Twitter:

The establishment of a "province" in a region where it has nothing resembling actual governance is absurd, but it should not be written off…The world may roll its eyes at these developments (I sure have), but to jihadists in these vulnerable regions, [these] are significant gestures to help lay the groundwork in rebuilding the map of the ISIS "Caliphate." Thus, these regions should be closely watched.

Kashmir alone shouldn't be considered as the only fertile ground for seeding a quasi-state utopia.

Most terrorism in India, the 2008 Mumbai attacks, for example, has been related to the India-Pakistan or Kashmir conflicts, or to a longtime territorial struggle by domestic Marxist guerrillas. India hasn't been a target for global jihad in the way Europe or the United States have. But neither had Sri Lanka, until the Easter bombings killed more than 250 people there, and ISIS claimed responsibility.

Sri Lankan authorities probing those 2019 Easter attacks have expanded their investigation to southern

India, where officials say the alleged mastermind of the bombings had traveled. It's also where one of his followers was arrested in late April, accused of planning another suicide attack. Experts believe Sri Lanka, south India and the Indian Ocean region may get conceived as the new front for global jihad.

A joint team of the IB and RAW attempted to trace the whereabouts of 22 Indians who fled the country and were suspected to have joined the ISIS in Afghanistan in the year 2016. These Indians, hailing from the Kasaragod and Palakkad districts of Kerala, had left the country, and were possibly de-neutralised after the US dropped a GBU-43/B Massive Ordinance Air Blast (MOAB, also known as the 'Mother of All Bombs') in the mountainous regions of Afghanistan's Nangarhar province, targeting the ISIS Khorasan Province and its fighters. The interrogation of these captured operatives was enlightening to the department. The message was clear: the threat of an Indian Ocean region front was very real.

A proto-state can be established not just by turban-clad Pashtuns but also by educated extremists who identify themselves as a separate sect that is ideologically non-conformist or messianic, and that in any way finds itself absolved of the rule of the existing establishment. These sects can constitute a sophisticated network of intellects, teachers, writers or even militia. The success of the LTTE in Sri Lanka still beckons many similarly ambitious groups all over the world.

And it's not always religious fundamentalism or sectarianism. It could be other western ideologies such as liberalism, nationalism, communism, democratic socialism and even fascism that motivate the sense of a distinction and a yearning to break free. There were areas in Naxal-infected states where Maoists ran their own governments. Areas where the police or paramilitary forces could never enter owing to them being siphoned off from the ruling regime's control by their own Maoist army, called the People's Liberation Guerilla Army.

No matter what form they take, once ANSAs establish near-exclusive control in an area, they tend to become authoritarian and non-pluralistic, ruthlessly resisting any conformist groups or the mainstream in general. Mezzanine groups and their leaders lack any kind of culture of accountability, and their need for regular income makes them prone to corruption and organised crime. It is often difficult for counterinsurgency forces to distinguish the criminal from the politically motivated.

Anarchism, which in the modern world is yet another cult idea, can be defined as something that attempts, "at fundamental changes in the structure of society and particularly the replacement of the authoritarian state by some form of non-governmental co-operation between free individuals". It condemns the very concept of the State for its denial of the sovereignty of the individual. Anarchism, however, is a very fringe idea in India, although it needs to be kept under watch as there can always be cross-breeding of thoughts between different rebel viewpoints, in which one might identify commonalities to facilitate a unified doctrine while the other provides the logistics for execution. Naxalism is a classic example of a consorting of the minds of the intellectual writer and the landless peasant and is discussed elsewhere in the book.

The spread of modern communications technology has eroded one of the historical advantages that governments have had: control over information. State-controlled media used to allow the government to present only what it found palatable. But global interconnectedness, through satellite networks and the relatively ungoverned space of the internet, encourages ideas to spread across national boundaries.

India being as diverse a nation as it is, the sprouting up of sectarianism is inevitable. It has become much easier for people to be brainwashed into joining and empowering such groups. Thanks to unregulated connectivity, the state of affairs is such that non-state actors can brainwash and recruit members from any community, and establish a quasi-regime, a sect, right under the nose of the ruling establishment, without once having to venture into mainstream politics or even give a public appearance before its followers.

Many communities, especially minorities, view the ruling elite as stepmotherly and corrupt. They are seen as having supremacist and suppressive agendas. Distrustful of the government, people turn to their mezzanine rulers to safeguard their interests and living standards.

This, in turn, allows ANSAs to argue that the very weakness of the state necessitates and legitimises their existence and modes of operation.

It's a losing game for the state, not only due to the constant necessity of surveillance of activities of suspected individuals or groups. Irregular warfare conflicts that involve non-state armed groups will become the primary mode of fighting in the future, with urban areas in littoral zones as the main battlegrounds. The increasing relevance of armed non-state actors in contemporary and future conflict makes the study of their infrastructures particularly important for intelligence agencies around the world.

The IB needs to keep tabs on the sentiments trending in the populace, especially among the marginalised sections of society and in the more unruly remote corners of certain states. Propaganda mechanisms of any cults or sectarian groups as well as their funding sources need to be very closely watched to gauge their potency.

TWELVE

CYBERSPACE

While replying to a question in the Lok Sabha in November 2019, the Minister of State asserted that the government can lawfully monitor information, citing Section 69 of the IT Act, 2000. He further said that the government was empowered to lawfully intercept, monitor or decrypt information stored or transmitted on any computer for security reasons for the sovereignty and integrity of India. The minister further added that 10 agencies have been authorised to carry out such interceptions. The agencies are the IB, Narcotics Control Bureau (NCB), Enforcement Directorate (ED), CBDT, DRI, CBI, NIA, RAW, Directorate of Signal Intelligence (for service areas of J&K, the Northeast and Assam only), and the Commissioner of Police, Delhi.

Besides the limited information openly available, the IB and other intelligence organisations can track social media profiles, devices and locations. On August 13, 2018, the Central Government was compelled to withdraw its proposal of creating a social media hub through which it could monitor the social media accounts of citizens, following public cry and an objection from the Supreme Court. But it was a fact that even before the proposed plan of the Government of India, several of its agencies had been using tools to conduct mass surveillance of citizens and social media activists. The tool Advanced Application for Social Media Analytics or AASMA could collect 24x7 live data of users from multiple social networks, including Twitter, Facebook, YouTube, Flickr and Google. It could track social media profiles, posts and networks to identify users. According to the National Police Commission, police departments have been using this tool to find the location of criminals and other suspicious people.

Here, it is worth giving a bird's-eye view of the infamous ISRO spy case. India had to develop its own cryogenic engine and the task was given to ISRO scientists. There was reason to believe that the American CIA wanted to stall India's missile program. For this reason, two scientists who were directly involved in the cryogenic engine programme were reportedly implicated and brought out from the programme.

Later, a conspiracy was believed to have been hatched to subvert the programme, and it was suspected that a political angle was given to the episode to settle scores with political opponents within the ruling party. Though the Supreme Court of India exonerated the scientists involved in it, many in the IB and the state intelligence of Kerala continue to harbour the belief that there did exist a spy ring and that the case was diluted at the insistence of the highest-level government machinery. Cyber surveillance was one of the major tools used by the IB in this regard to investigate the spy case. The personality cult and professional ambition of certain senior officers both in the

IB and state police brought embarrassment to the IB in this episode. The tug-of-war between senior officers in various government departments is an open secret.

The Central Bureau of Investigation (CBI), the premier investigation agency in India, was in turmoil when it booked its own crooked officer for allegedly accepting Rs 2 crore as a bribe to sabotage a probe against a controversial meat exporter. The CBI also booked a senior RAW officer for fixing the deal between the CBI officer and the businessman. It also arrested a middleman on October 16, 2018. Senior CBI officials confirmed this unprecedented development and the registering of a First Information Report (FIR) in this regard. Allegedly, the deal was brokered by the RAW officer for Rs 5 crore and the CBI special wing intercepted a conversation that indicated that Rs 2 crore was already paid. This episode was highlighted by the media and ultimately the then CBI Director who initiated the booking of his subordinate was removed from the office by the government in order to save the guilty party, who was close to the ruling government. In this case, the IB was also interested in the removal of the CBI Director as some junior IB officers who were on routine surveillance were taken into custody by the CBI as the IB officers were found 'loitering' in front of the residence of the CBI Director.

The dark web and the malevolent power of social media

On January 17, 2001, loyalists of the Philippine Congress voted to undermine key evidence that testified against the Philippine President Joseph Estrada, when his impeachment trial was underway.

Within hours of this decision going public, thousands of angry Filipinos, converged on Epifanio de los Santos Avenue, a major crossroads in Manila. Fearing the prospect of the corrupt president being let off the hook, the protestors quickly mobilised the crowd, by broadcasting a text message that read, "Go 2 EDSA. Wear blk." The crowd explosion continued, and in the next few days, over a million people arrived, choking traffic in downtown Manila.

The public tenacity in coordinating such a massive and rapid response so overwhelmed the partisan legislators that they retracted their earlier decision and allowed the evidence to be presented. This moment was a big blow for Estrada. Unprecedented, as for the first time, the people had gotten the better of him. The crowd power had arm-twisted his trusted lackeys to abandon him, their leader; by January 20, he was gone. The event marked the first time that social media had helped force out a national leader. Estrada himself blamed "the text-messaging generation" for his downfall.

In the lead-up to the 2004 presidential election in Ukraine, supporters of Viktor Yushchenko, then the leader of the opposition, used text messaging to organise the massive protests that became the Orange Revolution. All these were the beginning of the realisation of the power of social media.

Since the rise of the internet in the early 1990s, the world's networked population has grown from the low millions to the low billions. Over the same period, social media have become a fact of life for civil society worldwide, involving many actors—regular citizens, activists, nongovernmental organisations, telecommunications firms, software providers, governments.

The troll armies and smear campaigns

The Russian interference in manipulating public sentiments during the US elections in 2016 is the most recent example of the power of media and if this has had the effect that conspiracy theorists claims it has had (something that is increasingly getting confirmed by the American intelligence agencies), then this might have been the greatest act of subversion and manipulation of a democratic process by a hostile nation. The next leader of the most power nation in the world might have just been decided by another nation, and a hostile one too. This goes to show the impact that such simple soft tactics can produce.

The investigations by American intelligence agencies concluded that Russian President Vladimir Putin personally ordered the covert operation. The Internet Research Agency (IRA), called the troll farm of Russia, allegedly created thousands of social media accounts that appeared to be Americans supporting radical political groups, and planned or promoted events in support of Trump and against Clinton.

The activities of these fake accounts reached visibility of millions of social media users between 2013 and 2017. Fabricated articles and disinformation were spread from Russian government-controlled media and promoted on social media. Additionally, computer hackers affiliated with the Russian military intelligence service (GRU) infiltrated information systems of the Democratic National Committee (DNC), the Democratic Congressional Campaign Committee (DCCC), and Clinton campaign officials, notably chairman John Podesta, and publicly released stolen files and emails through DCLeaks,

Guccifer 2.0 and WikiLeaks during the election campaign. In addition, funding to Trump was also procured by shell companies which had their true owners in Russian capitalists. There were massive content posting campaigns that selectively targeted Hillary Clinton with damaging information pertaining to her.

As the communications landscape gets denser, more complex, and more participatory, the networked population is gaining greater access to information, more opportunities to engage in public speech, and an enhanced ability to undertake collective action.

"Information technology has demolished time and distance". "Instead of validating Orwell's vision of Big Brother watching the citizen, [it] enables the citizen to watch Big Brother. And so the virus of freedom, for which there is no antidote, is spread by electronic networks to the four corners of the earth."

Walter Wriston, the former CEO of what is now Citigroup, in 1997.

This spread of the 'freedom virus' here is made to sound like a liberating and emancipating phenomenon, with people breaking away from the shackles of autocracy with the knowledge gained by suckling at the teat of random crowd wisdom on social media. In this view, the spread of the "freedom virus" gives ordinary citizens tools to build alternative sources of power. The democratisation of communications, the theory goes, will herald the democratisation of the world.

Freedom and choice are terms that inherently have a certain *je ne sais quoi* to the free world. There seems to be an undeniable connection between freedom and the right to and choice of information on the internet. The introduction of the internet into an authoritarian country shares something fundamental with the advent of elections.

The question that remains unasked, however, is what unregulated internet freedom can do to an existing democracy. Applied on an autocracy it brings forth democratisation; what are its effects on a community that already enjoys democratic freedom? What happens when the tenets of freedom are increased beyond what is already available in a democratic setup?

Any romanticism of all this being an intellectual awakening is far from the truth, especially in the case of democracies. Cyberspace in reality can be a very dark place. In *You Are Not a Gadget*, Jaron Lanier argues that the anonymity provided by the internet can promote a "culture of sadism," feeding an appetite for drive-by attacks and mob justice. It has also enabled improvised acts of violence against communities and has been instrumental in proliferating the formerly occult viewpoints of the fringe few.

Imagine a secessionist group mind-conditioning a section of the community to change their perception of the ruling establishment. Imagine radicalisation using social media. What is even worse, imagine an external interferer. Imagine acts of terrorism, coordinated hate crimes managed solely by social media message broadcasts. Social media can very well act as the ether that touches all, flows into every home, is seen by every eye, and the popular acceptance of any information provided by means of technology as the indisputable truth just complicates the situation even further. The government has on multiple occasions found itself losing the allegiance and respect of its people overnight, thanks to an unregulated internet.

The fact to be understood is that when it comes to political critiques, civil sensationalising and propaganda, there is no place for the truth on the internet or any kind of open-source media for that matter.

China can take control of this; we, as a democracy, cannot. Authoritarian leaderships like that of China, have been to a great extent able to ensure that the increasingly free flow of ideas and information through the cyberspace fuels the economy without threatening their political power, in other words, by carpet bombing all network bytes containing any voice of dissent. According to a report on Democracy and Cyberspace by political author Ian Bremmer:

In June, the Chinese government released its first formal statement on the rights and responsibilities of Internet users. The document "guarantee[d] the citizens' freedom of speech on the Internet as well as the public's right to know, to participate, to be heard, and to oversee [the government] in accordance with the law." But it also stipulated that "within Chinese territory, the Internet is under the jurisdiction of Chinese sovereignty." That caveat legitimates China's "great firewall," a system of filters and re-routers, detours and dead ends designed to keep Chinese Internet users on the state-approved online path.

The Chinese leadership also uses more low-tech means to safeguard its interests online. The average Chinese Web surfer cannot be sure that every idea or opinion he encounters in cyberspace genuinely reflects the views of its author. The government has created the 50 Cent Party, an army of online commentators that it pays for each blog entry or message-board post promoting the Chinese Communist Party's line on sensitive subjects. This is a simple, inexpensive way for governments to disseminate and disguise official views. Authoritarian states do not use technology simply to block the free flow of unwelcome ideas. They also use it to promote ideas of their own.

India ideologically cannot approve of these means for curtailing the free thoughts of its citizens.

But the problem remains that these technologies provide access to information of all kinds, information that quench a wide range of human appetites — from arousal to rationalisation, from hope to anger.

They provide the user with an audience but do not determine what he will say. They are a megaphone, and have a multiplier effect, but they serve both those who want to speed up the cross-border flow of information and those who want to divert or manipulate it.

The medium fuels many passions — consumerism and conspiracy theories, resentment and fanaticism. Militants and hate groups of various kinds use the internet to recruit new members and disseminate their propaganda. ISIS's exploits on the internet and social media brought to the forefront the power of social media to mobilise the likeminded or convert the vulnerable populace. By the time the social media giants like Facebook acknowledged the problem and took restrictive actions, a virtual Islamic State thrived boisterously in cyberspace.

Intelligence gathering in cyberspace through cyber-surveillance is the only way ahead. This would mean embracing technology solutions to neutralise a technology-based threat. Counter-extremism agencies are in dire need of new and innovative ways of uncovering digital indicators. Machine learning and deep learning technologies, albeit currently futuristic thoughts, might provide solutions here. Radical right-wing as well as leftist posting behaviours should be detected with a great level of confidence and analysed by the IB as a continuous process. Innovators have proposed methods for radical score assignments to posts on the internet. Using a sample of approximately 1 million posts and 26,000 unique users across four Islamic-based discussion forums, this study proposed a method of identifying the most radical users on the Dark Web. Novel algorithms such as the Sentiment-based Identification of Radical Authors—SIRA, originally envisioned by the trio of authors Scrivens, Davies and Frank R, can be a potentially beneficial acquisition for democratic governments, as in the case of India.

Cyberterrorism: Attacks on critical infrastructure

Although cyberterrorism does not entail a direct threat of violence, its psychological impact on anxious societies can be as powerful as the effect of terrorist bombs. A 2010 report on cyberthreats in a climate of escalating risk, argued that the increasing globalisation of the world, with its greater reliance on the internet and heightened dependence on computerised automated systems, represented a massive and escalating vulnerability—particularly with terrorist organisations finding alternative methods of assaults on governments and civilians.

Critical infrastructure describes the physical and cyber systems and assets that are so vital to the country that their incapacity or destruction would have a debilitating impact on physical or economic security or public health or safety. Attacking such infrastructure is possible if these are connected to local WANs or the web itself. Such cyber-attacks cannot hence be disregarded as mere annoyances but should be considered a threat to national security.

The Estonia attacks of 2007 are a fantastic case study to discuss. The country faced a massive attack. Suddenly, the country's vital infrastructure came crashing down. All this without one sign of who the enemy was. No bombs exploded. No one invaded the country. From newspaper websites to banks to power systems, everything collapsed. The massive cyber-attack campaign created chaos all around for 22 days. Perhaps the most prevalent attacks were distributed denial of service (DoS) attacks, resulting in temporary degradation or loss of service on many commercial and government servers. While most of the attacks targeted non-critical services like public websites and e-mail, others concentrated on more vital targets, such as online banking and DNS.

Per a post mortem report of the event, written by Rain Ottis of the Cooperative Cyber Defense Centre, Estonia, titled 'Analysis of the 2007 Cyber Attacks Against Estonia from the Information Warfare Perspective' it was clear that the cyber-attacks were linked with the overall political conflict between Estonia and Russia, a glaringly clandestine act of subversion by the enemy.

The malicious traffic often contained clear indications of political motivation and a clear indication of Russian language background. For example, malformed queries directed at a government website included phrases like "ANSIP_PIDOR=FASCIST" (Mr. Ansip was the Estonian Prime Minister at the time). Dozens of variants were used, often containing profanities.

Instructions for attacking Estonian sites were disseminated in many Russian language forums and websites. These instructions often included motivation, targeting and timing information, as well as a specific description for launching attacks. An example of these instructions is displayed in Figure 1. Note that this excerpt includes information about when, what and how to attack. It also illustrates how simple the most primitive attacks are to organize, provided you can motivate enough people to execute these simple instructions. With thousands attacking, even a primitive ping flood can cause trouble.

На 9-е МАЯ планируется повтор данной акции!
Не дай унизить своих соотечественников, отомсти за издевательства !!!
@ адреса eSSтонских депутатов

Программа для рассылки писем
(пароль на RAR: nnm)

Нажми (пуск -> выполнить -> cmd)
введи ping -n 5000 -l 10000 эSSтонский_сайт -t . и жми ENTER ВСЕ !!! Твои пламенные приветы полетели...
пример: ping -n 5000 -l 1000 www.riik.ee -t
Это 3 элементарных действия, после которых многие эстонские сайты просто перестанут работать!!!
Или вот .BAT файл, который в автоматическом режиме последовательно пингует эстонские DNS и MAIL сервера. Цикл бесконечен :)
Скопировать (красным) нижеприведённый текст, вставить в блокнот и сохранить как priveteSStonia.BAT (название можно любое) файл
(ты можешь сам добавлять адреса)

An excerpt of the attack instructions found on a website during the event.

Source: ccdcoe.org

Such attacks are usually conducted by a well-coordinated army of hackers, state-sponsored or non-state, but with a common passion to embarrass a nation, steal sensitive information or cripple its vital assets such as security or energy installations, telecom, transportation or even banking systems.

As per the latest information, hackers from North Korea targeted a nuclear plant in Tamil Nadu in India. A non-profit intelligence organisation in South Korea has shared "evidence" claiming that the attack on the administrative network of the Kundankulam Nuclear Power Plant was conducted from North Korea. According to the Issue Makers Lab (IML) the NGO claimed that the North Korean hackers targeted several nuclear scientists, including former members of the Energy Commission and Atomic Energy Regulatory Board, using self-branded computers produced and used only in North Korea. The IP used by one of the hackers was from Pyongyang. North Korea has been interested in thorium-based nuclear power, which is to replace the uranium nuclear power as India is a leader in thorium nuclear power technology. Since last year, North Korean hackers have continuously attempted to obtain information, the IML claimed. Nevertheless, the Department of Atomic Energy (DAE) spokesperson only informed the press that considering the sensitivity of the matter, the DAE would check the veracity of such reports. Interestingly, the DAE did not either deny or support the claim.

The IML further claimed that North Korea's Kim Suky Group had attempted to steal information on the latest design of an advanced heavy water reactor (AHWR), an Indian-designed for a next-generation nuclear reactor, that burns thorium into the fuel core. Given India's vast resources of thorium, a successful development of AHWR technology could significantly alter the potential of civil nuclear power in India. The South Korean Intelligence

Group has been making revelations about North Korean hackers through a series of tweets since October 2019.

Sometimes the attack is aimed to confuse and manipulate, to affect the decisions and actions of an opponent.

In an article about possible Chinese strategies for invading Taiwan, Wu (2004) points out the possibility of using the information age equivalent of the concept of people's war. In the context of cyber-attacks, this means that ordinary citizens of a state can be motivated to use the resources under their control to independently attack enemy systems in order to confuse the defenders. Amidst all the noisy and ill-coordinated attacks, more professional intrusions can then be carried out, supplemented with physical attacks to take out the command and control systems of the opponent. (Wu 2004)

Cyber-attack strategies are easily designed to resemble a namesake people's war, since anyone can launch such attacks and hence the culpability can be spread.

The beauty of disguising such a planned assault as a people's war is that it allows for absolute deniability on the part of the agency that sponsored the attacks.

In 2010, India was the third-worst-affected country by the computer worm Stuxnet. According to reports, of the 10,000 infected Indian computers at the time, 15 were located in critical infrastructure facilities. These included the Gujarat and Haryana electricity boards and an offshore oil rig of the state-owned petroleum explorer ONGC. The Supervisory Control and Data Acquisition (SCADA) system websites have been reportedly accessed by various terrorist organisation members in order to gather intelligence on these potential targets. SCADA systems are used to monitor and control utility equipment, such as power and water distribution systems. Control over the SCADA system by a hacker can be deemed highly impactful, almost as disruptive as attacking key sectors of the economy that are driven by computers, such as banking or telecommunications.

As was seen in a recent report in the Economic Times:

Chinese firms have bagged SCADA contracts for more than 18 Indian cities. Companies such as Harbin Electric, Dongfang Electronics, Shanghai Electric and Sifang Automation either supply equipment or manage power distribution networks in these cities. This becomes particularly a cause for apprehension since China is increasingly being seen as a possible source of any future threat to India's critical infrastructure.

The amount of foreign influence in component manufacture for such critical infrastructure is worrisome. The Ukrainian power grid attack is something that needs a special mention. Hackers around the world appear to have been testing the most evolved specimen of grid-sabotaging malware ever observed, so as to gain access to the victim nation's utilities networks and manually switch off power to electrical substations, causing a blackout that can last for weeks depending on the effectiveness of the contingency strategy of the nation to isolate and ring-fence the spread of the malware.

In August 2017, the government directed 21 smartphone makers, most of which are Chinese, to inform it about the procedures and processes they follow to ensure the security of mobile phones sold in India, following reports of data leakage at a Chinese telecom company. In addition, the government is also planning to create a new tri-service defence agency for cyber warfare. This Defence Cyber Agency will work in coordination with the National Cyber Security Advisor. It will have more than 1000 experts who will be distributed into a number of formations of the Army, Navy and IAF.

THIRTEEN

MONEY LAUNDERING, HUMAN/DRUG TRAFFICKING

Most of the threats to the nation, be they terrorism, subversive activities, armed rebellions, corruption, secessionist movements, externally controlled actors or narco-terrorism, all have one thing in common. They all need constant funding to thrive and they all leave a money trail.

In other words, they are all money-driven. Even when the motivation can be out of true passion for the cause (extremist passions are often aroused and proliferated using social media and the cyberspace), it still needs money. Most criminal and terrorist organisations use laundering to funnel funds from illegal enterprises through legitimate businesses. These act as a smokescreen to conceal the identity as well as the destination of the money. Track the money flow and one can stumble upon most of these criminals on the way. The IB can benefit a lot by never taking their eyes off the money realm. All funded or profit-generating crimes are bound to leave their footprints in the money realm at some point. All one needs to do is track the disruptions or anomalies in the flow of money. The 'dirty money' industry is the source of power that all these crimes feed off. It is, in many ways, the mother of all evil.

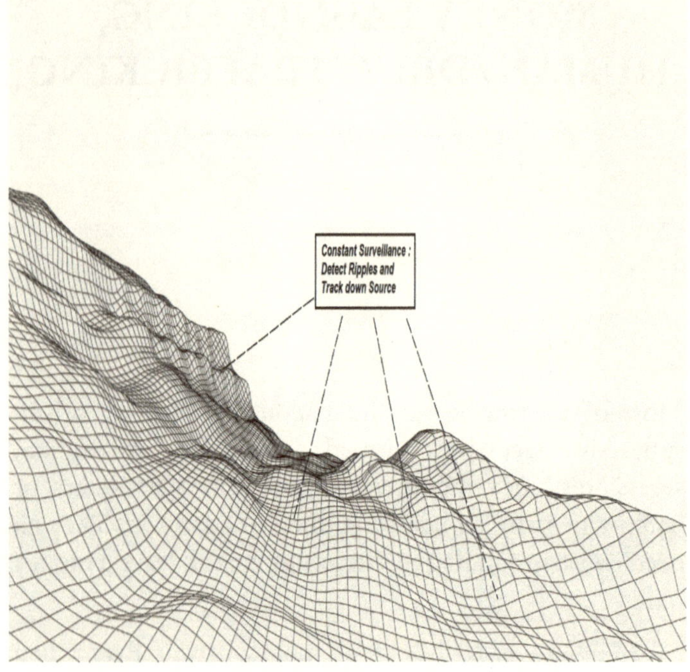

All criminal activities are bound to create ripples in the fabric of the cash-flow realm or the cyber realm. They invariably leave their trace. Modern-day intelligence strategy should be to detect anomalies in these realms, and then track down the threat that is being fed by the transactions in the cash-flow realm or the propagandas in the mediacyberspace. Technology will play a pivotal role in this.

Money laundering is an inherent requirement of organised crime. It is an aspect that is intrinsic to any profit-generating criminal activity. Modern-day governments around the world have taken cognisance of this fact and have been investing heavily in anti-money laundering controls. This could be through bank regulations or civil legislation. The creation of the Financial Action Task Force (FATF), an independent inter-governmental body that develops and promotes policies to protect the global financial system against money laundering and terrorist financing was a way forward in this regard.

Money laundering is the illegal process of concealing the origins of money obtained illegally by passing it through a complex sequence of banking transfers or commercial transactions. The overall process returns the money to the launderer in an obscure and indirect way. This accounts for the proceeds without raising the suspicions of law enforcement agencies. It is indeed a sophisticated financial strategy and once the money has been laundered it can be used for seemingly legitimate purposes. Some countries define obfuscation of money sources as money laundering, whether they are international or merely using financial systems that do not identify or track the routes or destinations. Some other countries define money laundering in such a way as to include money from activities that would have been a crime in that country even if the activity was legal where the transaction occurred. In short, it is a very complicated system that makes it very difficult for law enforcement and intelligence agencies to detect, investigate and get the culprits punished in a court of law.

Vijay Kumar Singh, Professor of Law, says this about money laundering:

"Many instances of money laundering would have the tint of an international flavour as money laundering typically involves transferring money through several countries in order to obscure its origin. Man can use money as a tool for good and bad."

In short, laundering refers to the conversion of money which is illegally obtained so as to make it appear to originate from legitimate sources. Money laundering is used by launderers worldwide to conceal criminal activities associated with drugs, arms, terrorism and extortion. Money laundering is not an independent crime. It depends on other crimes.

Most crimes have a counterpart in the handling of funds, often embarrassingly large amounts of money, which must somehow be legitimised.

Here the role of intelligence agencies, particularly the IB and RAW, come into the picture.

According to India's Prevention of Money Laundering Act, 2002, a money launderer is, 'Whosoever directly or indirectly attempts to indulge or knowingly assists or knowingly is a party or is actually involved in any process or activity connected with the proceeds of crime including its concealment, possession, acquisition or use and projecting or claiming it as untainted property.'

The US Money Laundering Control Act of 1986 made money laundering a federal crime. It directed banks to establish and maintain procedures to ensure and monitor complaints with reporting and record-keeping requirements as per the act.

The Financial Intelligence Unit-India (FIU-IND) was set up by the Government of India on November 18, 2004, as the central national agency responsible for correcting, processing, analysing and disseminating information relating to suspected financial transactions. FIU-IND also coordinates and strengthens the efforts of national and international intelligence, investigation and enforcement agencies in pursuing global efforts against money laundering and related crimes. FIU-IND is an independent body reporting directly to the Economic Intelligence Council (EIC) headed by the finance minister.

The Prevention of Money Laundering Act, 2002, which was enacted in India on January 17, 2003, was aimed at preventing money laundering and confiscation of property derived from or involving money laundering. The Act provides for punishments with rigorous imprisonment from 3-7 years, besides confiscation of properties in any form.

High-profile financial scams where money was laundered out of India:

1. The Commonwealth Games scam 2010, in which Rs 70,000 crore was involved. Out of the Rs 70,000 crore, only half of the amount was spent on Indian sports. Charges were levelled against organisers, traders or non-existent parties for wilful delays in the execution of contracts, overinflated prices in the purchase of equipment and misappropriation of funds. The large amount of money was laundered to make it look legal.

2. The Punjab National Bank (PNB) scam: A fraudulent letter of undertaking worth Rs 11,600 crore (USD 1.77 billion) was issued at a branch of PNB in 2018, making the bank liable for the amount. The fraudulent transactions were linked to Nirav Modi, who is presently stationed in Britain. The case is under investigation and attempts are being made to bring the culprit back to India through legal channels to face prosecution under Indian law.

3. The Saradha Group financial scandal, 2013, involving Rs 4000 crore, caused by the collapse of a Ponzi scheme run by a consortium of 200 private companies that were believed to be running collective investment schemes such as chit funds.

4. The coal allocation scam, 2012: Estimated to be worth Rs 1,85,591 crore. The Controller and Auditor General of India unearthed a huge loss to the exchequer as the allocation of coal blocks was not auctioned as per existing norms. This case was brought before the Supreme Court of India which eventually cancelled the allocations since 1993.

5. The 2G scam, 2008, involving Rs 1.76 lakh crore, in which 2G telephone licenses were issued to various companies at lower rates than the market values. The then telephone minister and others were in jail for a few months in this case.

6. The Yes Bank money laundering case in which several business tycoons were involved. It involves over Rs 4300 crore.

7. The Kingfisher fraud involving over Rs 9000 crore has been in the news for more than four years. The banks in India, including the SBI, advanced the amount to Kingfisher Airlines, but so far, no way has been found to recover it. Cases are pending in both Indian and foreign courts. Kingfisher argues that this was a business failure rather than fraud.

In India, the annual income generated from the illegal drug trade, one of the largest criminal enterprises, through extensive transportation and distribution of drugs to affluent European and US markets facilitates the generation of black money, which has political social and historical dimensions. The unholy nexus between politicians and bureaucrats on the one hand businessmen on the other, fuels black money and its laundering, creating a black economy in the country.

Ever since the media exposed the involvement of huge amounts of money from drug trafficking in 1989, the general public has been familiar with the expression 'money laundering'. The estimated money laundered in India as part of global drug trafficking is worth around 500 million USD.

At a recent Economic Summit, the Central Vigilance Commission (CVC) estimated that black money accounted for 40 percent of the GDP. According to a study, in India, the *hawala* system is used extensively for drug trafficking and remittances of money by both non-resident and resident Indians. In India, 8 percent of black money has roots in crimes such as bribery, drug trafficking and terrorist activities. The other 92 percent is from evasion of taxes.

Money laundering has an impact on businesses, economic development, social problems, etc. With regard to its social impact, the possible social and political costs of money laundering, if left unchecked, are serious. Organised criminals could infiltrate financial institutions; acquire control of large sections of the economy and, ultimately, the government. This could weaken the social fabric, ethical standards and economic and democratic institutions. A great deal can be done by the government to combat money laundering. Some of these tools are enacting acts for the agencies in exchanging information within and outside. India has more than ten acts enacted to counter criminal activities including the Prevention of Money Laundering Act, 2002 (PMLA), the Prevention of Terrorism Act, 2007 (POTA), The Conservation of Foreign Exchange and Prevention of Smuggling Activities (COFE POSA) and the Foreign Exchange Management Act (FEMA).

Terrorism and money laundering

Terrorist financing in India as well as in the subcontinent is linked to the *hawala* system. The involvement of Indians in the underworld of the international diamond trade is also a major threat to be dealt with by various agencies, particularly the IB. The present Financial Intelligence Unit (FIU) is to be fully operational with the greater involvement of the IB in order to disseminate suspicious transaction reports and further governmental action.

Terrorism has become a part and parcel of money laundering and the IB has been contributing to detecting it through timely collection of intelligence fed to the competent authority.

The IB has perhaps the best interrogators, particularly to interrogate terrorists, religious fundamentalists, counterfeit currency dealers and connected global troublemakers. Whoever is caught on suspected activities is invariably interrogated by specialised IB sleuths who extract and elicit the maximum information possible. This information is then passed on to prosecuting agencies like the police, FIU, ED, CBI, Income Tax, etc. The menaces of counterfeit currency, money laundering and related crimes have the capacity to generate high profits and are often linked to all other types of crimes, including subversion by foreign interference. Experiences and interrogation reports identify the money laundering and terrorist financing vulnerabilities and risks of the diamond pipeline. The diamond trade is subject to considerable risks. The closed and opaque nature of diamond markets and the value and ease of carrying diamonds, combined with a lack of expertise on the part of the enforcement agencies have led this industry to becoming susceptible to abuse by criminals.

Hawala: The unregulated money exchanges

The FATF has this to say about hawala:

In South Asia and Middle East, the word hawala is commonly used to refer to "Pure Traditional Hawala", a centuries-old money transmission system which was often used for trade-finance. These systems have operated for centuries in an unregulated environment. Pure Traditional Hawala and other similar service providers are also extensively used to send low-value remittances on behalf of individuals, for example, migrant workers—extending outside their historical geographical area as populations migrate and trade routes develop. For instance, hawala are a common provider for remittances to migrant workers in the United Arab Emirates, where a significant portion of the working-class population is composed of expatriates. Pure Traditional Hawala and other similar service providers tend to be popular among migrants because of familial, regional or tribal affiliation and inadequate access to regulated financial services for senders/recipients in origin/ receiver countries.

According to a study by the FATF conducted with globally diversified cases, a spate of case studies on the matter of hawala were received from various countries on their perception of how criminal hawala operates in their geography. The two studies below are the case examples that were provided by India from the various real scenarios that have been observed here in relation with Hawala and Other Similar Service Provider (HOSSP)

Case Example 1: Terrorist Abuse of HOSSPs

In a case of hawala money transfer to terrorists of the proscribed terrorist organisation X in India, two hawala operators along with two receivers of hawala money for the terrorists were apprehended in the year 2011 and an amount of approximately INR 2,000,000 (USD 32,000) was recovered from them.

They revealed that the hawala money was provided by the organisation leaders based in country Y and routed through another country Z where another over-ground worker of the terrorist organisation is based. The modus operandi is that the terrorist leader in country Y collects terror funds in that country and sends it to another terrorist agent in country Z, who contacts hawala operators who operate freely in that country.

Apparently hawala is not illegal in country Z. The hawala operator in country Z then gives a number on a currency note to the agent along with the telephone number of the person who would deliver the money in India. The agent then informs the terrorist leader at Y.

The terrorist leader at Y then contacts the over-ground worker of the proscribed terrorist organisation at Delhi and provides the telephone number of the hawala agent and the number of the currency note.

This over-ground worker then contacts the hawala operator at the given number and collects the money at the decided location after giving the number of the currency note. The over-ground worker does not get to know the identity of the hawala operator as he delivers the money wearing a scooter helmet.

Note: The terrorist agent does not have to pay any commission at the receiving end.

Case Example 2: Terrorist Abuse of HOSSPs

In another case of terrorist financing, a sum of INR 10,000,000 (USD 160,000) was intercepted in State A in India which was meant to be delivered to a terrorist gang X.

Investigations revealed that a number of earlier consignments had earlier been delivered to the terrorist gang earlier. It was revealed that development funds of a particular area in that state were defalcated and then sent to location P in that State. From location P, it was sent to location Q in another State B with the help of hundi operators operating between State A and State B. The hundi operators are told that the money belongs to a very influential person in state A

The hundi operators do not object conducting the transaction when they hear the name of this influential person and deliver the money at State B to the person authorised by the agent of the terrorist gang. The money is delivered after deducting a commission of 1 percent from the total money which is transferred.

Contd,

At State B, the hawala money is then changed from rupees to dollars in an unregulated exchange market and then transferred to another country E, where arms and ammunition are purchased by the terrorist gang leaders based there. These arms and ammunition are then transferred across the borders and then delivered to the terrorist gang operating in State A for carrying our terrorist activities. In this case a total of 15 accused were arrested and chargesheeted and the trial is being held. The arrested members include terrorists, contractors and agents.

The problem occurs when the lack of regulation and supervision over the changing of hands in case of a hawala system makes it susceptible to being abused by launderers, most importantly for terror financing or for transmitting the proceeds of drug trafficking.

These setups enable the transmission of funds with little or absolutely no Customer Due Diligence (CDD) rule adherence. The CDD rules require certain identity audits, beneficiary traceability and customer risk categorisation norms to be applied when opening bank accounts. These and other related KYC norms by themselves exert a great degree of control on shell companies and non-existent made-up beneficiaries on either side of a money transaction. Unregulated hawala means the absolute absence of these, thereby allowing a money launderer or terror financier to freely send funds without the risk of being identified.

As hawala is such a multifaceted genre, regulating the sector becomes a very complex issue. The major roadblock is the ability to segregate between the pure money remittance systems that hawala traditionally has been from criminalised hawala. Overregulating pure hawala would mean imposing on it the same governmental controls and money exchange complexities that came across as tedious to the minds of the daily wager and the migrant, which had themselves led to the concept of hawala as a simpler system for transferring money across different geographies.

This would push hawala as a whole to become a completely underground operation and almost fully facilitated by those who are understand the underground, the criminals.

On the other hand, the ever-increasing restrictions and strict AML (Anti-Money-Laundering) obligations being enforced by more and more countries in the regulated financial realm have made the unregulated hawala framework an extremely attractive alternative for transmitting dirty money.

A common standardisation and regulatory enforcement may not be the most efficient system when it comes to hawala. This then leaves it to constant surveillance by the IB as the best option to track, trace and bust criminal operations at the back of hawala-based funding.

Diamond trading and money laundering

In the recent years, countries around the world have begun to recognise that diamonds and precious metals as vehicles for laundering the proceeds of crime.

The overvaluation of diamonds is usually the modus operandi in these cases. The diamonds are exported at a much higher value than their real or market value.

This kind of overvaluation cannot be done for goods with a fixed or even relatively fixed price.

With precious stones and metals, it is possible to do this owing to the extremely high value of the commodities and the fact that there aren't really verifiable or even stable prices for these. Imagine diamonds being exported with an invoice showing prices as exorbitant as USD 24 million while the net worth based on the true per carat value isn't even USD 100,000. These get past customs checks owing to the ambiguity of their true pricing and the end result is the diamond trader's account transacting millions in laundered money.

The risk of such laundered money being used for further criminal purposes like terrorism is not something that can be written off.

Human trafficking

Human trafficking is the criminal trade of men, women and children for the purpose of forced labour, commercial sex or other forms of exploitation. The potential to generate sizeable financial returns makes human trafficking a common crime for money laundering. There are over 40 million global victims of human trafficking and it generated up to USD 150 billion in 2018. The proximity between human trafficking and money laundering means that financial institutions play a crucial role in its detection and prevention, provided the financial institutions are aware of the complexities in the system.

Human trafficking takes numerous forms, through coercion, fraud or force. Traffickers often move the victims between locations across international borders. The three main types of human trafficking are as follows:

A. Human trafficking for the purpose of prostitution or other sexual exploitation

B. Human trafficking for forced labour or slavery

C. Trafficking for the purpose of removal of organs for the organ trade business

There will be better opportunity for identifying signs of money laundering from human trafficking if the offender or victim is exposed to the financial sector, such as through opening a bank accounts or other registered business.

Money laundering stages

According to the definition given by the Board of Governors of the Federal Reserve USA, (2002), money laundering is a dynamic three-stage process that requires:

1. **Placement**: Moving the funds from direct association with the crime;

   The placement stage involves the physical movement of currency or other funds derived from illegal activities to a place or into a form that is less suspicious to law enforcement authorities and more convenient to the criminal. The proceeds are introduced into traditional or non-traditional financial institutions or into the retail economy.

2. **Layering**: Disguising the trail to foil pursuit;

   The layering stage involves the separation of proceeds from their illegal source by using multiple complex financial transactions (e.g., wire transfers, monetary instruments) to obscure the audit trail and hide the proceeds. Funds can be transferred through multiple banks domiciled across a mix of jurisdictions in order to blur the trail to the source of the funds.

Sometimes wire transfers are made from many accounts, into which deposits have been made by cautiously distributed multiple small transactions from a principal collecting account, often located abroad in an offshore financial centre.

3. **Integration**: making the money available to the criminal, once again, with its occupational and geographic origin ns hidden from view. During the integration stage, illicit earnings are mixed with clean money. This is done by giving a makeover to dirty money to make it resemble legitimate business earnings through normal commercial activities.

Source: unodc.org

Funding methodologies

Understanding the diversity of funding for armed non-state actors can help states (or other non-state actors) develop policies and improve strategies in dealing with sub-state militant groups—by way of negotiations, sanctions against host states and industries, or armed engagement.

Natural resources are an intuitively lucrative source of income. Those like fossil fuels, and narcotics, which are in ample supply and high demand, only reinforce this notion of profitability. Controlling large amounts of territory also presents opportunities for fundraising. Not only does land provide organisations with more natural resources, it also encompasses populations from whom money can be extracted, by means of taxation or otherwise.

Investment into and proceeds from natural resources can refer to oil, gas, coal, sand, or can include other resources as diamonds, rubies, and, most importantly, narcotics and human slaves.

It all depends on which industries an organisation can control or, at the very least, can influence, to redirect the proceeds to their primary activities.

External support, like natural resources, is a highly lucrative source of income. Unlike natural resources, outside patronage is not geographically limited and is (potentially) inexhaustible. Different external actors fund secessionism and terrorism for different reasons. Most often this funding is out of geopolitical consideration. Though they seek alignment with their ideological or religious principles, repressive, interferential or territorial goals are usually the primary thought. External funding also comes in the form of non-state donors, such as wealthy individuals and organisations. Ideological, religious, and territorial ambitions all contribute to the external sponsorship of organisations.

FOURTEEN

NON-GOVERNMENTAL ORGANISATIONS

NGOs as the new arch-manipulator and the homewrecker

An NGO is supposed to be a non-profit engaged in humanitarian activities, independent of governments, and is active in education, healthcare, public policy, social causes, human rights, the environment and other areas to effect changes according to their respective objectives. They are funded by citizens, or at times by government and foreign aid.

The superpowers of today, including the US and other Western powers, power elites with a globalist agenda, have made interference in and influencing of the policies of other sovereign nations a key attribute of their foreign and security strategy. NGOs have become one of the manifestations of **soft power** by which the West can manipulate and dominate a country without firing a single bullet, or even declaring war or accepting any aggression on their part. These contenders for 'leading the New World Order' can just go about making their influence felt and subverting events in weaker target nations, while remaining in the shadows.

On the surface, **NGOs** usually appear very benign, pro-freedom, humanitarian and 'blue-helmeted'. They have achieved for themselves the reputation of being the champions of the commoner and the poor, activists against repression and totalitarianism, protectors of the planet and fearless voices that expose the schemes of 'the man', 'the ruling class' and 'the crony capitalist'.

Many do perform genuine philanthropic work. However, many NGOs are conceptualised right from their origin as a control mechanism for the funding nation, as their instruments of infiltration and influence. This subterfuge and veiled deceit have gone on unregulated for a long time, but now, in the aftermath of the 2014 Ukraine coup and other events, nations are beginning to wake up to the trickery and illicitness that can be intrinsic to the very concept of NGOs.

The NGOs use soft power to influence public sentiment and stealthily disseminate external propaganda among the masses.

In many cases they seduce people with the dream of a utopia that they claim exists elsewhere. The indoctrination conditions people's minds and prompts in them a leap of faith, a shift of allegiance. People start resenting, in many cases unjustifiably, their own politicians, and force them to make policy changes, usually favouring the external parties who have been shadow-funding the NGOs.

The soft power wielded by NGOs has become more and more apparent to governments around the world now and restrictions have begun on their earlier uncharted funding.

In July 2016, Israel passed a new 'Transparency Bill' requiring foreign NGOs to declare the sources of their funding. The law enacted will force human rights groups that receive more than half their funding from abroad—including from European governments—to disclose it prominently in official reports.

The introduction of the law read: "The law wishes to deal with the phenomenon of NGOs which represent foreign interests of foreign states, while acting under the cover of local organisations seeking to serve the interests of the Israeli public;" and Israeli Prime Minister Benjamin Netanyahu said the law's goal was "to prevent an absurd situation in which foreign states meddle in Israel's internal affairs by funding NGOs, without the Israeli public being aware of it." Earlier, in December 2012, Russia passed a law that was specifically targeted against US NGOs operating inside Russia. In March 2015, India, too, banned 69 NGOs from receiving foreign contributions, 30 of them being minority- and missionary-oriented.

The restrictions that are enacted by any country primarily fall under these categories:

♦ Activities of NGOs participating in political activities or implementing other activities constituting a threat to the interests of the country and receiving funds from foreign citizens or organisations to be suspended and their assets seized.

♦ Citizens with dual citizenships to be prohibited from membership or participation in the management of NGOs or in the political activities of the country.

♦ NGOs under the scanner to lose rights to found mass media outlets and to be restricted from conducting mass and public events.

Occupy Central Hong Kong

The impact that the Occupy Central NGO in Hongkong has had in galvanising people with its civil disobedience campaign was testified to in the 2014 and later 2019 Hong Kong protests. This time around China has been the target of a US-run sabotage initiative. NGOs such as NED, or National Endowment for Democracy, and NID, National Democratic Institute, both part of the colossal NGO network of the mega-donor George Soros, have been alleged to have played a large part in all this. Soros has previously been alleged to have used his many NGOs to act as de facto arms of Western intelligence agencies and governments, and his NGOs have played a central role in the destabilisation of multiple regimes, including China, to a great extent in recent years. The US State Department is said to be directly funding the NED and the NID. The result of all this is that Hong Kong government is losing political strength in maintaining its legitimacy and the social cohesion that it once had with mainland China, while preserving the high degree of policy autonomy that it previously enjoyed. It is in tatters and is left trying to pick up the pieces and trying to re-consolidate the thriving democratic model that it previously presided over. Consequently, the governing capability of the Hong Kong government is decaying, and its political strength is deteriorating. On the flipside, China has become extremely wary of sabotage attempts by the West in a region that is of utmost economic importance to it. China considers this a covert assault against its perceived hegemony in the region, even to the extent of looking at it as interference in its internal matters. It tolerated all the free-Tibet mania that had engulfed the thoughts of the socialites and the celebrities of the West, but with Hong Kong, a nerve was struck. China is been trying to and probably has already succeeded in retaliating.

Not being as good as the West in passive manipulation and subversion, China might have become desperate when confronted with the possibility of losing Hong Kong's allegiance. This panic might have led it to darker realms of more sinister ploys used in proxy wars, one of them being biological espionage.

The timing of the onset of the global pandemic Covid-19, originating, most probably, in a Chinese lab, raises great suspicion. This is more elaborately discussed in the chapter on biological espionage. These thoughts at the moment can only be categorised as conspiracy theories and someday in the near future, a widely acceptable truth might come out. But if that truth points towards any mischief on the part of China with regard to increased activity with virology experimentations and deliberate or inadvertent spreading of the virus, then the Hong Kong protest angle will have to be understood as a primary motivator.

A threatened, cornered animal was not to be expected to have responded in any other manner.

The planning of the Hong Kong protests, the mobilising of the masses, the arrangement of the sit-ins, all took place owing to a failure on the part of Chinese intelligence to correctly gauge the power of NGOs and understand their funding and secretive affiliations.

The Ukraine coup

The Ukrainian coup of 2014, aimed at a regime change there, was allegedly orchestrated and sponsored by George Soros' NGOs, which were pumped with more than USD 5 million for the job.

Kiev's Euromaidan was thronged by demonstrators, many of them members of Soros-funded NGOs or, in some cases, trained in the workshops and conferences conducted by the International Renaissance Foundation (IRF), and various other Open Society foundations, all connected to Soros' network of brazenly US-funded NGOs. These member activists, who even included some former government servants, allegedly appealed to the battalions for their allegiance to the people rather than the ruling regime. The military men were assured that their cooperation in the matter wouldn't go unrewarded when the new government assumed office.

The IRF, which was founded by Soros in the aftermath of the coup, claimed that it had given more than any other donor organisation to what it calls the democratic transformation of Ukraine. As in the case with China, Russia, too, responded ferociously and annexed the Crimean region of Ukraine in early 2014, in the aftermath of the Euromaidan revolution.

Nevertheless, it is an entire arsenal of NGO soft power out there, indirectly controlled by Western donors and government departments and they now form part of the passive foreign strategy of these governments. Their use is now on the rise to facilitate the covert projects of psychological manoeuvring and perception shaping. Interestingly, if we study the history of the involvement of humanitarian and peace-keeping NGOs through the various regional conflicts, we can see that the positions taken by the NGOs were always fully aligned with the Western stand on the matter. This could have been a remnant effect of the Cold War-era subversions, in which the NGOs active in the ex-Soviet Bloc were naturally allied with the West or were in many cases conceived by the West. These NGOs kept their loyalties to their western patrons intact even after the Cold War.

In the Balkan War of the 1990s, the human rights organisations ironically enough supported the sentiment of Balkanisation, which was what originally started the bloodshed. They pushed for a regime change when the West wanted it, rather than pushing for the best option that would have immediately restored peace, whether the Syrian war of the Libyan crisis.

The US and the West have used the NGO-based subversive tactics in anger against whomever they considered a threat. It cannot be written off that these tactics won't get used against India and these tactics are reproducible by anybody, not just the West. China is getting better at it now with its growing influence in world organisations and with it entering the funder's league for these non-profits, the WHO being a recent example. Increasing Chinese funding in these organisations is surely a new threat, since it denotes its attempt to become a bigger player in the soft power games.

NGOs in India

Although India and the US have been allies for the most part of modern history, US interference in Indian affairs has always been a matter of apprehension, and rightly so.

India has nearly 20 lakh NGOs—that is almost one NGO per 600 people. They continue to receive millions of dollars from the US and European countries.

NGOs play a vital role in India and are easy channels for foreign intelligence organisations to send their spies undercover and to pump huge amounts of money into the country.

There was once a time that the Soviets had a lot of leverage in India, particularly the media. Recently a former KGB agent revealed how the KGB prevailed upon Indian scientists, bureaucrats, journalists, professors, research scholars, NGOs and political parties during the time of the erstwhile Soviet Union through Indian communists to slow down various developments in India.

Similarly, the CIA virtually arm-twisted India not to give asylum to Edward Snowden, the former CIA agent who leaked 1.7 million classified documents from the CIA relating to massive surveillance by the US. The flow of CIA money to Indian NGOs, in which many men of influence are deeply connected, has indeed motivated Indian leaders to formulate new policies.

The flow of foreign money into India became uncontrollable and the government had to enact a law known as the Foreign Contribution Regulation Act (FCRA) in 1976 in order to regulate the flow of foreign money. The task was given to the IB and it has a separate FCRA wing to monitor the activities of foreign-aided

NGOs with special reference to their anti-Indian activities. Whenever an NGO would like to receive foreign aid, it has to get prior permission from the Ministry of Home Affairs (MHA) and the IB must clear it and recommend FCRA registration. Though many NGOs are genuine and do good service among the needy and marginalised sections of society, many are found to be fake and money-earning establishments. Not to mention the instances of entry by foreign spy agencies through these NGOs for their covert and ulterior motives. It is also to be noted that some NGOs are floated at the will of a few bureaucrats and politicians in the names of their spouses or close relatives as chief functionaries. These are mainly aimed at siphoning off donation money to personal accounts, and not particularly at subversion, but unknown to these NGO owners, these too, could be used for activities and propaganda that can inflict harm to the nation. This makes it necessary to keep a tab on all the financial dealings of these NGOs as well.

The nation's intelligence needs to extremely cognisant regarding the activities, both apparent and disguised, that are undertaken through such externally controlled NGOs. To that end, the IB has been keeping a close watch on all NGOs that are under suspicion and their foreign donors, and recommends actions, including the cancellation of the FCRA, if the NGO is found engaged in anti-national activities.

Master of Intelligence. Using Our Nation's Intelligence Faculties

REAL AND PRESENT DANGERS TO THE ESTABLISHMENT AND THE NATION

There have been mounting complaints and criticisms from opposition parties ever since the system of democracy rule began in India and these are expected to increase. During the time of the Congress-led government, the BJP and its allies accused the Centre of misusing the intelligence agencies and the police force for political gains, saying that it could jeopardise national security. Later, opposition parties vehemently criticised the BJP-led government for misusing the IB, RAW, CBI, Narcotics Control Bureau, ED, Income Tax, and other agencies to suppress the Congress and all others who oppose the government. Many self-proclaimed intellectuals and social activists express their concerns over a range of issues that are threatening the Indian polity.

Constant violence, religious fundamentalism, state vs. centre and state vs. state tension, inter-caste disharmony, economic reforms, secessionist movements and various other threats emanating from India's border are the main factors disturbing India's society. Many anti-establishment forums, including certain NGOs and the press and electronic media, level accusations that the modern Indian state seems to be returning to a monarchy.

'With the body of ministers proved upright by means of secret tests, the King should appoint in secret service the sharp people, the seeming householder, trader and secret agents, the poison-giver and the begging man'.

The Arthashastra

Like the false loyalists and Macedonian sympathisers who threatened Chandragupta Maurya's rule back in the 4th century BC, a new set of internal and external threats are on the increase in India and, consequently, the relevance of intelligence officers is also on the rise.

According to *Intelligence and National Security*, a book published by Frank Cass & Co., UK, another equally disturbing threat to the security of Indian citizens is the very way in which India's intelligence agencies function.

It also discusses the development and operation of India's intel agencies and evaluates the performance of the agencies not only from the perspective of their role in promoting India's legitimate national interests but also within the context of how they are increasingly utilised by the political authorities to maximise their vested interests.

Further, there are indications that intel agencies are seeking to set policies rather than reporting it to the authorities. The article further says that this trend represents a substantial threat to Indian individual freedom, civil liberties and the very democratic process itself.

K P S Gill is, undoubtedly, one of the best cops the country has ever produced, and to whom the country should always be grateful for completely smashing and suppressing the dangerous Khalistan movement. His knowledge of policing in this country will not be contested by any government. In the December 2012 issue of the Indian Police Journal, he wrote, 'No policing and intelligence apparatus can perform its functions with requisite competence if it is compromised by corruption or when its officers and personnel are mixed up with the very people they are meant to monitor. Nor can any intelligence system fulfil its mandate if it is constantly looking to please political masters by telling them what they want to hear rather than what is actually the case; or worse, when the agencies are directly involved in orchestrating political mischief. On some occasions, the consequences have been devastating to the national interest.'

People have a reason to believe that we are currently at one such moment of deviation from the national interest, which may at times be according to the interest of the ruling party.

Writing on the functions of Indian intelligence agencies, Ajay Sahini, Executive Director of the Institute for Conflict Management in Delhi, opined that the legitimacy and effectiveness of intelligence are best served when agencies make a clear distinction between the nation and the regime. But the fact remains that the nation is represented by a transient regime. Legitimate intelligence operations serve the interest of the constitutional state and are required to resist subordination to the partisan interest of a particular government from time to time. National interest, security and constitutional values are the touchstone against which legitimacy is to be defined.

Intelligence agencies discredit themselves by misdirection, by providing false, misleading and convenient intelligence to the expectations of the political executive for electoral and political manipulation. Some others are of the view that the IB reports start appearing in public nowadays at the insistence of the government.

This is a new trend that was unheard-of a few years ago.

Use of intelligence by the government

Despite the criticisms of the misuse of intelligence agencies by the ruling government, as the eyes and ears of the government, every democratically elected government has the right to the IB's services. One should understand that India is a democracy and the elected government has indeed the legitimate right to utilise the IB and other agencies in its favour during the period it enjoys a majority in Parliament. After all, the elected government represents the will and expectations of the people. The defence forces, the police and all enforcement agencies are under the control of the elected government and their job is to comply with and execute its decisions and policies. The agencies however have the option to advise the government about the constitutional fallout, the mood and temper of the general public and social and political implications. In India, we have a reputed judicial system to protect the law and the constitution if such policies and decisions are *ultra vires* to the spirit of the constitution.

Election assessments and the popularity and efficiency of possible candidates are invariably crosschecked and recommended by the IB at the instance of the ruling government and there is no harm in this exercise. The hue and cry against alleged political vengeance is often a futile proposition. This methodology is used in every democratically elected government around the world, including in India. Nevertheless, it is widely known to the public, and one cannot ignore the use of the IB, CBI, IT, ED and other agencies to unearth enormous amounts of wealth and black money from wrongdoers who are politicians, bureaucrats or businessmen.

Nobody could define these governmental actions as vengeance or a political vendetta, though on certain occasions, it stretches the limits. If the actions of a government are unacceptable to the majority of voters, it could be defeated in the next election. In a democracy, there is no other option left in this regard.

From the experience and expertise of the author, if a thorough and critical analysis is conducted, nearly 80 percent of the alleged misuse of intelligence and other agencies are found to be useful for the overall interest of the nation.

However, the remaining 20 percent could be unwarranted and undertaken with a view to setting scores with the opponents.

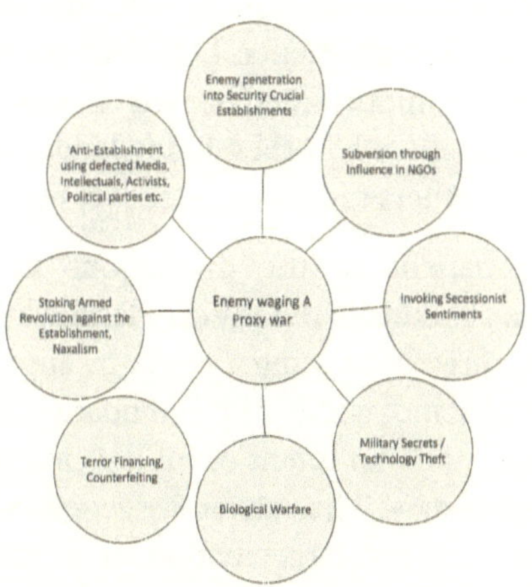

REAL threats that need intelligence time.

SIXTEEN

SUBVERSION AND THE OVERTHROW OF THE ESTABLISHMENT

Defining subversion

Subversion does not have one accepted definition. Like in the case of 'fundamentalism' or say, 'people's war', any attempt to define subversion will only leave a lot of loose ends and disagreements. Different nations agree or disagree on its definition based on what is more convenient for them, especially when they hold clandestine stakes in an activity that others categorise as subversive.

For the benefit of the discussions in this book, subversion can be considered any clandestine interventional action taken, directly or using a proxy, by any state outside its own bounds and within the boundaries of a separate sovereign state, with an intent of influencing the outcome of events in that state. The subversive actions can be aimed at either harming the target nation or influencing it to make decisions that in some way are favourable to the aggressor nation.

The Second World War ended with a divided Europe. The two remaining superpowers of the world that emerged out of the ruins of the ensuing cataclysm were poles apart in their vision of how the new world should look. For decades, there were two co-existing world orders, so it was somewhat of a precarious situation to say the least. Subversion and sabotage became the new rules of the game and the whole situation was given a name, the 'Cold War', since 'subversion', even back then, was as brittle and disagreeable a term as it is today.

While subversion today aims to control a limited territory of influence, during the Cold War, the US and the Soviet Union permeated the globe, and infiltrated foreign markets and social orders. American secret services remained concerned by communist and Trotskyist subversion. MI5 was extremely wary of the trade union movements that were gaining ground in the UK. Alleged communist sympathisers were witch-hunted from all walks of life in the western world, be it union leaders in the UK mining industry or movie producers in Hollywood. Churches denounced communism as ungodly; state propaganda humiliated any unionist political parties as 'Commies'.

For the Kremlin, too, the paranoia ran sky high of a US-led subversion on its own soil or within the boundaries of its European possessions. Both sides discredited any claim by the other of it having indulged in subversive tactics, but indulge they did, taking turns in painting the world red and blue.

The superpowers and their allies saw subversion as a useful part of their national security repertoire. They played most of their games inside weaker, lackey states, in the post-colonial 'Third World'.

A few cases of subversive actions that were manoeuvred by the Left, the Liberals and the Right are listed below:

- Through the 1950s and 1960s, the United States covertly introduced into Chile a variety of programmes and strategies ranging from funding political campaigns to funding propaganda aimed at impeding the presidential aspirations of a leftist candidate Salvador Allende. A whopping USD 3 million was spent on propaganda against Allende, who was considered the top contender during the 1964 elections. Print advertisements run by the CIA against him played a crucial role. Salvador Allende ran again in the 1970 presidential election, winning this time. This was intolerable to the United States, which was wary of Chile becoming another Cuba-like threat for them. The then CIA head Richard Helm's handwritten notes from an emergency meeting that was called by President Nixon said this:

  "1 in 10 chance perhaps, but save Chile!; worth spending; not concerned; no involvement of embassy; $10,000,00 available, more if necessary; full-time job—best men we have; game plan; make the economy scream; 48 hours for plan of action."

  The CIA: A Forgotten History: US Global Interventions Since World War 2: William Blum

  The plan thus formulated had a Track I, involving assistance to trade unionists, politicians and journalists, and a Track II, which was to nurture and support military officers and others who could mutiny against President Salvador. This track culminated in an externally invoked coup d'état in 1973, thus overthrowing Allende

♦ An audacious plan by three Harvard men (graduate student Clemens Heller, college senior Richard "Dick" Campbell and young English instructor Scott Elledge) in the summer of 1947 to rebuild post-war Europe intellectually and enable its reconstruction on a democratic basis, arranged for publication in the West, of the first Russian-language edition of Boris Pasternak's novel Doctor Zhivago. This 'Book Program' quickly grew in tenacity and distributed millions of copies of a wide range of western literature in the Soviet Union and throughout the Warsaw Pact countries (Soviet Union, Albania, Hungary, Poland, East Germany, Czechoslovakia, Bulgaria). Add to that, the CIA's covert support to the 'Congress for Cultural Freedom', a group of artists and intellectuals that promoted liberal, democratic alternatives to Soviet totalitarianism. By 1985, the seeds thus sowed yielded fruit. The very idea of the Soviet Union was set on a path to disintegration. A growing political ferment in the USSR forced Premier Mikhail Gorbachev to introduce two new policies: "glasnost," or political openness and "prestroika," or economic reform. What ensued was the tearing down of the Iron Curtain, the death of Soviet influence in Eastern Europe. By 1989, every other communist state in the region replaced its government with a non-communist one.

This was by far the most profound outcome achieved in history solely by acts of subversion and propaganda. One superpower had dismantled the other, turning the world from bipolar to unipolar. All turned out well in the end some might say, but this underlines the potential of something as stealthy and passive as subversion.

♦ An act of subversion that involved direct armament and inciting of insurgency was Operation Cyclone, the CIA program to fund and arm the mujahideen in Afghanistan from 1979 to 1989. A Marxist-leaning Democratic Republic of Afghanistan Regime, heavily under the Soviet influence, was simply unacceptable and the then US president Jimmy Carter decided to interfere. The programme leaned heavily on Pakistan's ISI being the middlemen in arms delivery to the rebels, along with handling their mentoring and training. Muhammad Zia-ul-Haq in Pakistan and his regime favoured the most hard-line fundamentalists among the various Afghan resistance groups fighting the Russians and this meant that most of the funding reached these groups.

♦ Soviet subversion was even more extensive and included the destabilisation of democratic governments in Central and Eastern Europe during the late 1940s. The Nicaraguan liberation movement Frente Sandinista de Liberación Nacional (FSLN) was founded in 1962 as a revolutionary group committed to socialism and to the overthrow of the Somoza family, who were considered US puppets. The Soviets' covert support to the group enabled a unification of the various Sadinistas in 1978-79 and paved the way for the Nicaraguan Revolution and its eventual success.

Indian diaspora: The Kashmir situation

The shaping of the Kashmir conflict through the late 1980s reeks of external subversion and mind conditioning. The idea was an ethnic cleansing of Kashmir, more precisely, disinfecting the region of the Hindu 'muqbirs' (informants to the Indian government), thus paving the way for the secessionist ambitions of the 'Plebiscite Front' (later named the Jammu Kashmir Liberation Front, JKLF). The group was conceived in Birmingham in the UK by Amanullah Khan in 1965. Amanullah later moved operations to the Pak-Occupied regions of Kashmir and played into Pakistan's hands in return for general patronage and funding. The organisation's unofficial armed wing, called the National Liberation Front, carried out sabotage activities in Jammu and Kashmir well into the mid-nineties. The role played by the JKLF (also called the 'Mahaz-i-Rishumari) in the forced exile of the Kashmiri Pandits irreversibly modified the demographic equation of the region, displacing around 600,000 Hindus from Kashmir. Kashmir was now a state with 97 percent Muslims, most of them tending towards the Wahabbi hard-line. Even the Sufi minorities were systematically neutralised. Pakistan's ISI put to full use both its 'Kashmiri liberationists' mentee the JKLF and the foreign imports, the Mujahideen (namely the Harkat-ul-Mujahideen and Hizbul-Mujahideen), who were spat out of the Afghan War and was kept reserved in Pakistan's militant arsenal. These groups moved into planned phases of threatening and blackmailing the Hindu population in Kashmir. The organised ghettoization of the Hindu minorities continued with the assassination of Hindu lawyers and businessmen. Propaganda ran amok and news dailies started to issue threats to Hindus to leave Kashmir immediately. Walls were covered with Islamic posters with verses on ultra-conservatism and puritanism that were to be followed. These called for conservative dress codes and restrictions for all women and bans on music and education, to name a few. Buildings and street walls were painted green to usher in the dawn of the Wahabbi vision of an Islamic State. Wahabbi orthodoxy contained within itself an irresistible magnetism for the Sunni youth, especially at a time when they yearned for a doctrine that could substantiate their sense of cultural segregation from the rest of Hindu India. The 'smoking out' of the Hindus took newer dimensions to whole new extremes when mosques allegedly started broadcasting diktats to Muslim men to fulfil their religious duty of sanitising the valley of infidels. All these in hindsight seem to have been merely threatening tactics to intimidate the non-Muslim. But the Kashmiri Pandits had received the message loud and clear and without any help seen to be coming from the then Indian government, they decided to undertake the exodus out of the valley.

The whole saga unfolded in a period of little less than five years, but the gravity and profundity of this change remained unfathomed at that time. This forced segregation of the masses created a division, a sectoring that could never ever be eliminated. Kashmir was, all of a sudden, a region of only one ethnicity, one religion, one sentiment, one dream and one allegiance. Kashmir had lost its pluralism forever.

Subversion, including by those using proxy warriors or non-state actors, has often been compared to non-violent terrorism. This is not entirely true and cannot be typecast across varying geographies. The Middle East and the Indian subcontinent especially, have seen armed assaults aimed at destabilising the ruling establishments or simply acting as an externally paid wound-inflictor or a general menace. Terrorism in these regions is invariably armed and martial in nature. But these ANSAs, being externally funded by an enemy nation, do not fall under the definition of a general people's uprising or a revolt, since very often even the troublemakers infiltrate from across the border. So, in such cases, terrorism funded externally should fall under the banner of extreme subversion, falling short of an all-out war only by virtue of the lack of an open declaration of war.

Subversion, especially manoeuvred by the Soviets or Maoist China during the Cold War era, would usually come across as passive before the eruption of the actual armed conflict.

The stages would usually be selection, indoctrination, propaganda, (or using other economic and social control tactics to physically or psychologically separate target populations from incumbent regimes), funding, material patronising, arming, training and then waging an armed rebellion against the host nation.

The Maoist insurgencies during the Cold War, be it the Viet Cong in Vietnam or Naxalism in India used the same methodology.

Analysts have acknowledged the importance of identifying and countering subversion during the early stages of an insurgency, since the failure to do so would give the movement a time advantage that would be difficult and costly for the incumbent power to overcome. The leftist insurgencies that once troubled the developing world have since been, for the most part, replaced by non-state threats consisting of religious extremism, holy warriors and ethnic separatists. These fighters are out there today not to bring forth a red revolution but for religion, separatism, sectarianism or simply material gain.

Categories of subversion

Subversive activities can be grouped into three categories:

1. Establishing front groups, penetrating and manipulating political parties

2. Infiltrating into the armed forces, the police, other security establishments and critical institutions of the state, as well as important non-state organisations

3. Sabotage by fanning anti-establishment fervour and creating civil unrest through demonstrations and strikes

Anarchy through subversion

As with infiltration, fomenting riots, organising strikes, and staging demonstrations can have a corrosive effect on the power, presence, and capabilities of the state. Such unrest is first and foremost an affront to governmental authority, and the failure to suppress it can have damaging political repercussions for the state by demonstrating that it is incapable of living up to its fundamental responsibility to maintain public order.

At the same time, however, overreaction by security forces can play into the hands of terrorists and insurgents by seeming to confirm the opposition's claims about the fundamentally repressive nature of the state. The death of a demonstrator at the hands of the Berlin police in 1967 helped radicalise a generation of German young people, who came to believe that the Federal Republic of Germany was the Nazi regime reborn—a key component in the ideology of subsequent terrorist groups, most notably the Red Army Faction (RAF).

Civil unrest can be useful in a myriad of political and operational ways. Disturbances on a large scale can decrease the resources of the state by forcing the authorities to deploy additional police, pay overtime, and in some cases send troops into the streets. With the security forces otherwise occupied, insurgents and terrorists gain a respite from the incumbent's campaign against them. Additionally, the greater presence of the security forces in response to unrest—in the form of patrols, roadblocks, and searches—can help the cause of the terrorists and insurgents by seeming to confirm the opposition's charge that the state has "militarised" the conflict and is now "at war" with people.

Subversion and provoking anti-establishment or secessionist sentiments along with armed rebellion remains among the greatest threats the country's national security is currently facing. However, the gravity of the danger imposed by these is usually hidden from the public eye. The media and the general masses are usually receptive only to the threats of outright cross-border insurgencies or religious terrorism as the prime inhibiters to national security.

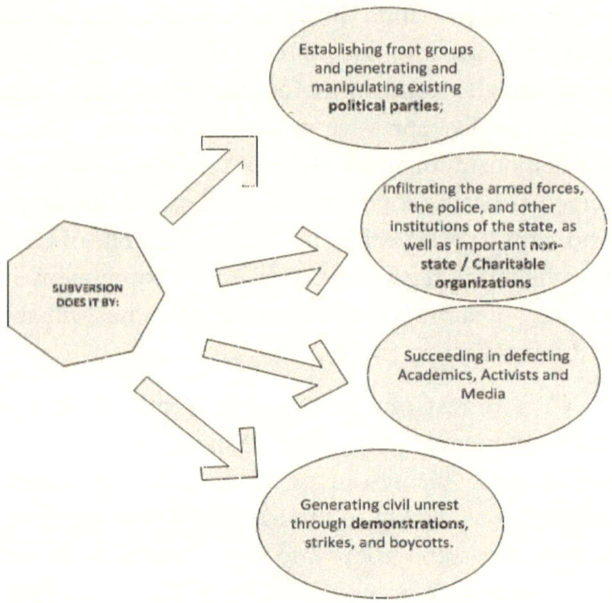

Subversion and sabotage initiatives by enemies are much more severe and prevalent in today's world. They flourish under the covers in society like a slow-growing cancer and weaken the nation exactly as they were conceived to do.

Analysis and control of these forces is and should be the primary use of the department. This might mean initiating surveillance on citizens as intellectuals, businessmen, activists or even politicians. This might mean auditing the funding of an NGO or a political party's expenditure in propaganda. We should understand that any ploy originating and controlled by external forces, and aimed at destabilising or even undermining the popularity of a government that enjoys a democratic majority, is an act of waging a proxy war against the nation.

The sabotage of an existing establishment or a department is only the first part of the plan before the enemy moves to the next phases, which might involve causing chaos or divisions among the people, thereby winning over more insiders to act on the enemy's behalf. The enemy can then torpedo political parties that can be its lackeys and would compromise national interests once in power. Anti-establishment, anti-nation and secessionist sentiments can be invoked in certain regions which the enemy can then leverage to negotiate in the international community that the wish of the people of the region is to secede to the enemy. This brings a threat of a demand for a plebiscite by voters who are conditioned and manipulated by the enemy.

The attack can be aimed not just at the government, but at democracy itself, something that we already saw in examples pertaining to the Cold War-era subversions.

The elected government has the right as well as the obligation to keep tabs on any such nefarious attempts by an enemy nation.

To that end, the IB is the primary tool the Indian government has at its disposal, with the power to know everything, to overhear each and every word spoken as it deems fit awarded to it when it assumes office. The IB was conceived as the eyes and ears of the ruler and so should it be used. People's privacy is important no doubt, but it is not more important than national security.

SEVENTEEN

THREAT TO THE HEAD OF STATE

"See how they lie in wait for me! Fierce men conspire against me…

See what they spew from their mouths-- they spew out swords from their lips, **and they say, "Who can hear us?"**

> – King David's lament in the Book of Psalms.

The threats to the head of state or the head of government are a matter of great concern. Whether in monarchies or republics, threats of assassination of the head of state, a crime punishable under the law as 'waging war against the state' in India, is of utmost importance. While in the USA, the quantum of the punishment for attempting to threaten any government official is five years of imprisonment, it is life imprisonment in the United Kingdom. The threat could be assassination, a bomb threat, contract killing, extortion, coercion, terrorist threats, etc. Abstract changes in the international environment such as the shift to unipolarity, the rise of globalisation and the sympathisers of terrorist nationals have redefined the sort of problems confronted by the policy makers, military intelligence and security agencies in the area of national security, which obviously include the safety and protection of the chief executive of the country.

The stability of states (state includes the heads of states) and societies today depends less exclusively on blocking the military, economic and ideological initiatives of a foreign power and more on supporting the integrity of members (Oxford Academic International Studies 2007) of foreign countries but also the internal members within the state machinery.

Political assassinations and coups d□état have occurred multiple times in history. Presidents and heads of state have been executed, eliminated and their regimes overthrown, and in most of these cases there was a major role played by vectors internal to their very establishment. There can never be an overthrow of the establishment, and an elimination of its head without help coming from within its sections. This is the threat of the internal enemy. Almost no head of state in history or at present can boast of a complete acceptance and support of his establishment, that there is not one dissenter, one silent loather in his office. It is not realistic to think that every person, even in his own party, every worker in his office, his armed forces or in the various realms of society personally approve of all of his policy decisions. His popularity can vary within separate sections of the society. Maybe he is not popular with the middle class, maybe his policies have irked the businessmen and owners of corporations. It's possible that certain geographies were in general opposed to him during elections and cannot accept him as their leader. It's possible that he is just loathed by a few just because of his very identity, his race or religion.

The people who run his office, people of his administration, people who have a close proximity with him, who probably are even his fellow party men can belong to any of these sections. They can be the revering or the privately disapproving. The solution to this problem is not in fumigating his vicinity and his entire administration of all probable disapprovers. However, extreme due diligence, surveillance and background verification by the security agencies is pivotal.

And this is not necessarily unhealthy. Disapproval of and disagreement with national policy decisions is every citizen's right. But it becomes the responsibility of the intelligence and security agencies to gauge risk elements and their proximity to the head of government. How deep runs the sentiment? How hostile is a region or a section of society? How close can they get to the leader? Will they press the trigger? These are the questions that needs constant re-evaluations.

And so, this one thing, protecting the life of the person who runs the government and the country is the single most fundamental responsibility of the intelligence and the security apparatus of the nation. There is no point in all their forays into international covert operations and their subversive victories overseas. It doesn't matter if they were able to pull off regime overthrows and whether they wield absolute soft power and can manipulate popular perceptions in another country, and that they dominate the shadow games played around the corners of the world. All this is pointless if the security agencies aren't able to fulfil this one paramount responsibility back home. The responsibility to protect the boss, the head of the government.

In November 1963, the celebrations hadn't yet ended at the CIA headquarters after they had successfully manoeuvred the ARVN (Army of The Republic of Vietnam) into staging a coup d'état and assassinate Ngo Dinh Diem, President of South Vietnam, when just two weeks after this act of subversion, they found themselves outfoxed, even violated, when none other than the President of United States is assassinated in what would go down in history as the greatest intelligence and security failure ever. Their fox games had found their way back home and had cost them the life of their president.

Political assassinations have been part of the social reality from the beginning of empires. Alexander the Great ascended the throne after his father was assassinated. Pausanias, one of the bodyguards of Philip II, killed him while he was entering the theatre of Aegae. Pausanias wasn't a paid assassin or an agent of the Persians or the Carthage empire or any other enemies of Greece at that time. He was a lone disgruntled individual acting fully on his own.

We shall delve now into real incidents of assaults on heads of the government. We shall focus on the Kennedy assassination especially because it has some varying investigative angles. It is shrouded in mystery even today, which means the truth can be any of the scenarios listed below. With its mindboggling array of theories, any of which can be the truth, it is a near-comprehensive list of case studies on the matter. Under each of the categories below, we will analyse the possible Kennedy assassination connection, as well as discuss other incidents related to the category.

Opportunistic traitors, political aspirants

Four and a half centuries after Rome was founded, Julius Caesar rose to the seat of the powerful consul. Years of military triumphs, especially his victories in the Gallic wars and most importantly the public support he enjoyed, had made him most powerful in Rome's second triumvirate. Caesar took over power establishing himself as the people's emperor. He was loved by his people, who were fed up of the corruption that had crept into the earlier Senates. The Senate had become an extremely corrupt aristocracy, and the senators had amassed boundless wealth, while Romans suffered in poverty.

Caesar's initiatives of distribution of land to the poor gave him acceptance. He loved his subjects and his people adored him as the saviour of Rome. His generals loved him, too. He was awarded , boundless power over internal and international policies, economics and irritatingly to some, powers over the Senate as well.

Rome thrived and grew under Caesar, who had set it on the path to the glory that it was to become. But among the very officers who would dine and dance with Caesar, supposedly advising him on state matters, were senators whose own power and influence were now impeded by Caesar's rule. One such close advisor, who secretly loathed Caesar, was Marcus Brutus. Caesar kept Brutus very close, treated him as a son and consulted him on all important policy decisions. Though hesitant at first, Brutus gave in to a group of rogue senators who called themselves the Liberators and were conspiring to assassinate Caesar. Brutus relented finally and became the mastermind for the assassination.

In the meantime, Caesar was busy extending Rome's reach from present-day Syria down into parts of Africa, over to Spain, most of France and all of Italy, unaware that he was being surrounded by snakes. The moment the conspirators waited for came on March 15, 44 BCE. At a Senate meeting held shortly before his departure for a military campaign, as many as 60 senators unsheathed daggers hidden within their togas and stabbed Caesar, the emperor, 23 times, till he lay dead in a pool of his blood. Shakespeare's depiction of the assassination scene in his famous play 'Julius Caesar' immortalised the phrase "Et tu, Brute" (or "You too, Brutus?") as the emperor's last utterance when he saw Brutus charging at him with his dagger.

What is interesting is that Caesar's most trusted generals, like Marc Anthony, were always suspicious of a certain senator Cassius to be harbouring aspirations for the Roman seat of power. But they never acted on it. Cassius later turned out to be the main conspirator. What would have been if Caesar's protectors had acted upon the intelligence they had on Cassius? This was inaction that changed the very course of history. The most powerful man on the planet was murdered not by a foreign enemy but by a group of his own establishment; all this while, his praetorians, the legions of his imperial bodyguards focussed on external attackers.

Yes, sometimes the greatest threat to the leader of the establishment is lurking silently within the establishment, simmering below the surface, like a snake in a bush, he waits for the opportune moment to strike.

There always are opportunistic traitors. In the Kennedy assassination, there are theories that suggest that Lyndon Johnson had been getting a little too restless with his wait to become president after Kennedy. Johnson was probably the most powerful man in Capitol Hill, when the Kennedy brothers stepped into public service.

He was the right-hand man of the previous president, Eisenhower, and had the carte blanche during the time. He had the senate majority and probably wanted to run for re-election. But the Democratic presidential nomination went to a much younger, less experienced John Kennedy. Initially Johnson wasn't in the list of running mates that Kennedy was preparing, but being a Texan, he could get Kennedy the southern states and this got him the offer for Vice President. He accepted and waited for the opportune moment for a re-election or for obtaining the nomination the next time. Two years into office, it was becoming clear that the Kennedys were there to stay. There wasn't a doubt in his mind now that the nomination for the next year, too, would go to Kennedy. But it was worse now: Kennedy had personally indicated it to him that this time around he would not be the running mate.

In 1963, things started taking a turn for even worse for Johnson. Senator John Williams of Delaware began investigating the activities of Bobby Baker, secretary to Lyndon Johnson. The investigations were leading them to Johnson's many muddled dealings. An insurance agent, Don Reynolds, was to depose in front of a secret session of the Senate Rules Committee. Reynolds held information pertaining to a suitcase full of money which Bobby Baker allegedly confirmed was a "$100,000 payoff to Johnson for his role in securing the Fort Worth TFX contract". Reynolds also held with him evidence of a $25,000 kickback that Baker received on behalf of Johnson in return for the contract to build the District of Columbia Stadium.

Johnson knew that something needed to be done quickly. Reynold's testimony would mean the end of his political career; he could forget about the Democratic ticket in 1964. He would be politically executed by the Kennedys.

As it happened, the testimony was getting recorded at the very instant the Kennedy motorcade took that fateful turn onto Elm Street. Kennedy was shot dead a few moments later. The testimony came to an abrupt end when the news about the president reached the office of the Senate Rules Committee.

Had Lyndon played his final card at the most felicitous moment? Right when the Senate Committee thought they had him, Lyndon shocked and overwhelmed them with his masterstroke. He was now their acting president.

Another example would be the 1977 coup staged by General Zia-ul-Haq in Pakistan. General Haq was specially handpicked by Pakistani Prime Minister Zulfikar Ali Bhutto to be made the country's next Chief of Army, passing over many other senior officers. Such an elevation to a top post of the country's armed forces held careful political planning by Bhutto. He saw Zia as firmly religious and an apolitical military figure. Zia's perceived distaste for politics made him the best bet to be handed over the army. What was expected of him was simple: an army that will ever be adjutant to the civil administration. And that is exactly where Bhutto's calculations failed.

In 1975, the Bhutto administration was combatting widespread dissidence in his own party as well as civil unrest, especially in the North-West Frontier Province (NWFP now Khyber Pakhtunkhwa) and Baluchistan intensified as civil liberties remained suspended after the ousting of secessionist provincial governments of the region by the Bhutto administration. The Bhutto government was facing the most tumultuous times and it depended on its various offices the most for support. Unknown to Bhutto, there were new aspirations taking shape in a few of his own main men, especially his new Chief of Army, General Zia-ul-Haq.

Bhutto announced fresh elections to prove the people's approval of him. A clear victory for his party in the elections was rejected by the opposition party, accusing him of rigging the elections. The political turmoil continued. The Prime Minster was being attacked from all fronts, even after he had proven majority support among the people of Pakistan. There were inter-party hostility and many were vying to take over power. Amidst all this, an absolutely unprecedented development disrupts the calculations of all these contenders as well as of Bhutto. In the wee hours of July 5, 1977, Bhutto's protégé and confidante, his own pillar in the Army, Zia-ul-Haq had taken over power in a coup d'état. Bhutto and his entire cabinet are arrested by Zia's military police. A baffled Bhutto tried calling Zia, but he couldn't be reached. Zia had been planning the coup for months; he had isolated Bhutto's loyalists and waited for the right time to make his move. Bhutto was executed in 1979.

Opportunistic traitors can be everywhere. Pakistan was plunged into martial law followed by an Army rule for a decade.

An astute intelligence agency that could accurately assess these risk elements was what could have saved the lives of these leaders, leaders who were elected by the people. In Kennedy's case, the elected leader couldn't be saved. In the case of Bhutto, the intelligence failure cost Pakistan democracy itself.

Homegrown conspiracies: Discontent within the establishment on policy and administerial decisions

The US back-ops, CIA's external hand had been successfully rigging elections, doing propaganda, staging coups d'état and manoeuvring psych warfare around the globe for decades.

They helped evacuate part of the Nazi intelligence machineries after the World War and used them against the communists. They meddled in European elections in Italy and France through the fifties, overthrowing autocrats and dictators or just about anybody who inclined towards the wrong side in the increasingly bipolar world. In the Philippines and Guatemala, they had successfully manoeuvred events. Then they got the Cuba assignment.

Operation Mongoose was launched. It had an annual budget of hundreds of millions of dollars. Hundreds of agents, tens of thousands of Cuban spies, hundreds of fake business fronts and shell companies for laundering money. They waged non-stop war against Castro. Industrial sabotage, crop burning—it was pure black-ops. Cuba, however, proved tougher to crack, considering it was essentially a state extension of the Soviet Union itself, and of great strategic importance to the USSR.

There was no way the Kremlin was going to allow black ops to take down Cuba. After the Bay of Pigs invasion by the US, which backfired and failed, and the ensuing Cuban Missile Crisis, however the Oval Office in Washington seemed to have undertaken retrospection of its earlier decisions. Talks of a complete reversal of the Cuban policy were in the air. The President reportedly wanted to end the continuing black-ops plots to assassinate Castro and even disband the external wing of the CIA. Forensic historian Patrick Nolan, in his book 'CIA Rogues and the Killing of the Kennedys' hypothesised that four of the top officials in the agency not only planned the assassination, but also actually fired the shots. These claims may be overstated, but there surely were sections within the establishment that were upset with Kennedy on his policy changes, especially after he made extreme personnel changes at the helm of certain departments.

When Kennedy was informed about the coup at Vietnam and Diem's murder, one of his generals later remembered that he "rushed from the room with a look of shock and dismay on his face." Kennedy had not anticipated Diệm's murder.

Kennedy wanted an absolute change in US policies towards the USSR, and he had found a probable friend in none other than the Soviet Prime Minister Nikita Khrushchev, the most powerful man in the Soviet. But their multiple attempts at initiating a peace process was strangled by their own respective establishments. Kennedy and Khrushchev had gone through many back-channel communications, hiding from their own governments because they both had become increasingly sceptical about the motives of their establishments.

In 1961, the National Security action memos 55, 56 and 57 were drawn up, that from here on forth the joint chief of staff would be wholly responsible for all covert operations and paramilitary operations during peacetime. This effectively ended the reign and autonomy of black-ops. These memos sent shock waves through the echelons of power in the administration.

It was a case of a head of state surrounded by disgruntled elements within multiple offices of his own establishment, offices that could successfully work in unison and in isolation from the rest of the establishment, if they wished to implement corrections. What the president lacked was a security agency, an intelligence division that could see the danger within the greyness of things, that could connect the dots in the randomness and sense what was lurking just around the corner.

Homegrown conspiracies: Corporations and other power circles

War businesses are extremely dependent on Washington's policies on overseas engagements. The budget cuts on the Vietnam War that Kennedy called for in March 1963 could have been what caused the wheels to start turning. Nearly 52 military installations in 25 states and 21 overseas bases were going to come under the budget cut. Vietnam War was churning out gold for these corporations and that flow of cash needed to be kept intact.

A defence budget cut just wasn't exactly something that the corporations could reconcile with their business plan. If anything, it was the exact opposite. Increased engagement and a full-blown war effort by the US in Vietnam what they were betting on.

Thousands of helicopters were lost in Vietnam every year. The Bell Corporation that used to manufacture those helicopters nearly went bankrupt, when the military had agreed to use their helicopters for Indo-China wars (Cambodia, Laos and Vietnam). The F111 fighters came from General Dynamics Corporation, a newly created joint venture back in the mid-fifties, which currently is the sixth largest defence equipment manufacture in the world.

Since the war began, the defence budget had been raised to USD 100 billion. The estimate was that it would cross USD 300 billion before the forecasted time of the war to end.

Kennedy wanted to end the Cold War in his second term. He wanted to call off the arms race and cooperate with the Soviets. He had signed a treaty with the Soviets banning nuclear testing.

Kennedy was doing everything that would have cut short the cold war and most importantly the arms race.

The arms race, the phenomenon that had converted many military equipment firms into huge corporations, was now at the risk of being called off abruptly.

During the elections, the Kennedy brothers had gone to the people with the promise to end the Indo-China wars and get their marines back home, that hundreds of billions of taxpayer money would not be used for fighting wars in faraway nations for causes that didn't even matter to America. That this mindless armament that had been ongoing for more than a decade will be brought to an end. People were fed up of the Cold War and they elected Kennedy since they wanted change.

Of course, everyone knows that election promises are just for shouting into the microphones and never to be acted upon. The power circles in Washington, too, would have assumed the same from him. But problems arose when Kennedy set off to actually fulfil those promises. This sent the power circles into a tizzy and they started teaming up for a common cause. Unusual bonds were being formed. There was whining, even protesting against the president, but in hushed tones and in closed quarters.

Defence contractors, arms corporations, big oil bankers—everyone could see that their profits were to drop suddenly, probably were even staring at bankruptcy. In all the scrambling around and confusion that ensued, probably someone stood up and actually said the words, spelled out something that was in everyone's sordid thoughts already. And a decision was taken that changes needed be made. Probably they reached out to an internal agency that had a similar vexation with the President. But it needed to be done in such a manner that, when it was all over, anyone in the power structure could avail full deniability. No compromising connections or interactions were to happen except at the most secret junctions.

And it all paid off in the end. On November 26, a day after Kennedy was buried, acting President Lyndon Johnson announced, "Gentlemen, I'm not going to let Vietnam go like China did. I'm personally committed. I am not going to take one soldier out of there until they know that we mean business in Asia." He signs National Security memo 273, which essentially reversed Kennedy's withdrawal policy. Lyndon had famously exclaimed: "Just get me elected, I'll give you the damn war!"

By 1964 the US Congress passed the Gulf of Tonkin Resolution, giving President Lyndon B. Johnson broad authorisation to increase US military presence. He ordered the deployment of combat units for the first time and increased troop levels to 184,000. The power circles needed Vietnam, and they had it now. For the next more than a decade the war raged on, killing thousands of Americans and transferred hundreds of billions of taxpayer money into company accounts of defence and oil corporations. Defence contractors got their profits, the middlemen got theirs.

They wanted the arms race to continue, and any future president who held office took the cue on who is actually running things at the top and what was expected of him if he was to remain in office. The arms race raged on for almost half a century, squandering billions.

A capitalist lobby allegedly could plot against and terminate the President, supposedly the most closely guarded man on the planet. A tough pill to swallow, but these are possibilities at the least, what-if scenarios, that can be learnt from. Internal enemies to the person running the government can come in any form. There can be strong lobbies in the government circles who can go to any extent to have their influence in legislation. There could be many vested interests involved, sometimes of very powerful people. The head of state should have the liberty to make his own policy decisions and it is his secret service, his intelligence agency that should closely watch the ins and outs of everyone around him, the friends he makes and the ones he loses. The intelligence should continuously conduct studies on the power lobbies, their connections with people in the administration and the extent of their influence. The Intelligence office should be aware of all power circles that exists and their approval of the head of the government or the lack of it. Close surveillance and continuous risk evaluation are key to achieving this.

External hand

Harvey Lee Oswald who was a known Communist and Russian sympathiser, could have been a KGB agent. He was in the Russian embassy trying to defect to Russia. Investigators later concluded that he was in Russia three weeks before the assassination. All this might point to Cuba or Russia or a collaboration to have pulled the strings on Oswald, while he pulled the trigger on that 6.5mm Carcano rifle. The CIA had attempted assassinating Castro numerous times, and after the Bay of Pigs invasion by the US, animosity between these two leaders had gone into extreme levels. In short, the gloves were off, and both the nations were in a mindless scrimmage to knock off the other's president. With the CIA and security agencies now focussed more on the Vietnam situation, had Castro and the KGB working in collusion gotten the opportunity they had been waiting for: the US president left back home as a sitting duck, for them to take aim and shoot? Whatever the case may be, security agencies fell short tremendously in gauging the risk factors in US.

Meanwhile, the CIA were triumphantly playing their subversive games overseas. They had zeroed in on their target and had finalised their strategy. They were going to tap into the simmering discontent with the south Vietnamese autocratic family of rulers, and they knew that the overthrow of Ngo Dinh Diệm was inevitable to push South Vietnam to take the North head-on. The Vietnam War wouldn't be possible with Diệm at the helm. He had to go. Diệm's mistake was making his regime pro-Catholic. Diệm's favouritism towards Catholics and persecution of South Vietnam's Buddhist majority led to the "Buddhist crisis" of 1963. The government shooting of protesters who defied a ban on the flying of the Buddhist flag had exploded the situation beyond repair and had damaged relations with the United States and other previously sympathetic countries, and his regime lost favour with the leadership of the Army of the Republic of Vietnam. The CIA seized the opportunity to have the ARVN stage a coup d'état and assassinate Diem. In what the ARVN and South Vietnamese saw as a positive regime change lay

CIA's murky scheme to push the country into decades of war for furthering the CIA's own south Asian agenda. The Diệm assassination is yet another perfect example of how an external force can oust and eliminate a president of a sovereign state.

Let us discuss the Anwar Sadat assassination. Sadat, the then president of Egypt, was assassinated by the Egyptian Islamic Jihad in 1981 during the annual victory parade in Cairo. The Islamic Jihad group was nurtured and enjoyed patronisation by many external jihad groups, including the Al-Qaeda. Egypt and Israel have had a long history of military conflict, including the Six-Day War and the Yom Kippur War in the seventies. The reason for the assassination was cited as the Egypt-Israel Peace treaty that Sadat and Israeli Prime Minister Menachem Begin following the Camp David Accords, 1979, in Washington DC. The Arab world in its entirety was enraged at any conceptualisation of peace with Israel. Sadat's signing of the treaty meant an Arab nation recognising Israel as a country for the first time. This led to the Arab world delineating Egypt, thereby giving a diplomatic move by the Egyptian President, aimed at furthering the national interest, an unwarranted religious colour.

Sadat's action did not necessarily indicate a betrayal of Egypt's interests. On the contrary, the treaty was a victory for Egypt by all means and had come after months of intense negotiations.

The main features of the treaty were mutual recognition, cessation of the state of war that had existed since the 1948 Arab–Israeli War, normalisation of relations and the complete withdrawal by Israel of its armed forces and civilians from the Sinai Peninsula which Israel had captured during the Six-Day War in 1967.

Egypt agreed to leave the area demilitarised, while it retained Sinai as its part. The agreement also provided for the free passage of Israeli ships through the Suez Canal, and recognition of the Strait of Tiran and the Gulf of Aqaba as international waterways.

Anwar Sadat had earlier struck Israel militarily in 1973, starting the Yom Kippur War just after he came to power. He led a surprise attack against the Israeli forces occupying the Egyptian Sinai Peninsula and the Syrian Golan Heights in an attempt to retake them after Israelis had occupied them from the time of the Six-Day War earlier. Sadat was hailed at the time as the "Hero of the Crossing" and a hero of the Arab cause. Israel started to respect Egypt then onwards, accepting it as a formidable force in the Levant. Egypt also gained a renewed political significance with the US and Europe.

Sadat was articulate in fusing military action with diplomacy. Egypt's diplomatic victory in regaining ownership of the Suez Canal after they were in loggerheads with each is extremely admirable. His new peace policy led to the conclusion of two agreements on disengagement of forces with the Israeli government.

Sadat was a seasoned politician and a statesman, and at the same time a warrior with a plan for the Arab cause and Palestine. He knew when to go to war and when to disengage and go back to the diplomatic platforms.

The extent of his statecraft and foresight is well evident in him inviting the evangelical pastor Billy Graham to meet him during his US visit. Sadat understood the value of creating a level playing field between Israel and himself when it came to garnering religious support in the western world. His reaching out made him acceptable within the evangelical Christians in the US, even while he was forging relationships with the Vatican. In 1976, the Pope pledged his help to him in achieving a just solution for the Palestine problem. This was a huge victory for Palestine, since this meant Christian sympathy was no longer reserved for the side that was non-Muslim. However, the PLO (Palestine Liberation Organization) viewed each of these actions (in fact, anything but a re-pursual of the Yom Kippur War with Israel) as betrayal of the Palestinian cause.

Extremist forces within Egypt as well as the rest of the Arab world couldn't understand any of this. The assassination was planned well, without doubt with external support and sponsorship.

The Egyptian Jihad front, secretly patronised by elements from within the League of Arab States, was recruiting military officers, while Egyptian intelligence always remained a few steps behind. The intelligence did make multiple arrests in the weeks leading to the assassination, which included many members in the El-Jihad, but they missed investigating further into information of the existence of a jihad cell within the military. The blind Sheikh Omar Abdel-Rahman of the Islamic Group was arrested two weeks before but the intel agencies couldn't extract the needed information on time: information about his hitman, Lieutenant Khalid Islambouli, still looming large and going about, meticulously effectuating final preparations before he would strike just days later.

Losing Sadat was Egypt's loss of its best chance to align both with the west as well as the Arab world and to establish itself as a reckonable, secular nation in the region, on the path to development and international engagements, even economically, thanks to the provisions of the Suez Canal.

It was probably even a loss for anyone who truly aspired for a sustainable solution, a peaceful respite, and justice for the Palestinians.

A deranged opposer

'There's [an] intrinsic notion that a peasant cannot strike down a king.

Many Americans found it hard to accept that President Kennedy, the most powerful man in the free world – someone they perceived to occupy a position akin to a king – could be eliminated in a matter of seconds by someone they considered a nobody.'

Author and ex-district attorney, Vincent Bugliosi, Reclaiming History: The Assassination of President John F. Kennedy

Probably it was just one maniac who planned and executed it all. Probably he was just destined for perpetual infamy. The Kennedy motorcade had to pass right under the very office building where he was employed and had full access to. The car that day had to pass under the window, without the bubbletop on, and was to remain in range of his rifle for a good 15 seconds, all the while giving him giving him a perfect shot at the head of the president from behind. Let's consider a scenario in which all this was written the way Harvey Lee Oswald had wanted. Everything, the entire universe, seemed to have conspired that day to reserve for Oswald his moment in history.

Although all this extremely inconceivable, let us for the sake of argument agree that a peasant did indeed strike down a king. But that will also need to be supplemented by extreme inefficiency on the part of the security apparatus.

Lee Harvey Oswald was a loner, a deranged Marxist who admittedly hated America. He had been in Russia in 1959 and had tried to renounce his American citizenship for a Russian one.

He had a record of being reckless and deranged. He was earlier in the marine corps where he was trained for three years and got qualified as a sharpshooter with the military rifle.

Oswald, a Dallas resident, was in fact under surveillance by the FBI in Dallas. However, the local FBI, strangely enough, did not inform the Secret Service regarding his presence in Dallas as a threat factor.

This was especially shocking considering the fact that the local FBI knew he was employed at the book depository which was right along the motorcade path.

Now, apparently the Secret Service hadn't informed the local FBI of the turn to Elm Street either. The result: a deranged military-trained sharpshooter lurked inside the book depository building on Elm Street, unscrutinised and unwatched, taking aim through an open window.

Oswald had earlier attempted to kill Major General Edward Walker earlier in April 1963. How could such a mad man, someone who was on the FBI's watchlist, be let loose in the vicinity of the head of state? How could such non-trivial information be deemed unworthy of sharing between the agencies? All this showed systemic failures within the security agencies, a breakdown in communication with such profound aftermath.

We have had lone actors succeeding in assassination attempts in India, too. Smt Indira Gandhi was assassinated by a member of her own security guards. Indira Gandhi's murder is regarded as an act of personal enmity that emerged out of religious fundamentalism and a maniacal reaction to the ordering of the storming of the Golden Temple. Operation Blue Star was a national policy decision, one that the country's leader had to take for the sake of national security. There were multiple warnings issued before the storming of the Golden Temple complex, which by 1983 had been converted into a fort for militants, led by Jarnail Singh. There were light firearms and semi-automatic weapons brought into the complex, and, only days before the storming, Jarnail's men had murdered the deputy police inspector of Punjab, while themselves remaining untouchable in the shelter of the religious compound.

The secessionist movements for an autonomous Punjab were at their peak and Indira, as the chosen leader of the nation, was obliged to take the difficult decision. The decision didn't have any personal motivation; it was purely a security decision. The Sikh vengefulness that ensued crept into the minds of many, including the Prime Minister's personal guards.

In this case, however, there were security agency warnings about the guards Beant Singh and Satwant Singh, but in spite of the reports, a decision, probably by the Prime Minister herself, was taken not to replace the guards for their religion based just on suspicion.

Security to the Prime Minister of India and others

In India, security is provided to some individuals who are deemed to be at high risk of being the target of an assault. Depending on the threat perception on the basis of a final report by the IB, the category is divided into:

1. Special Protection Group (SPG) provided to the prime minister of India. The SPG is a federal law enforcement agency under the Cabinet Secretariat entrusted with the task of protecting the PM of India and members of his/her immediate family. It was formed in 1985 with a multi-billion-rupee annual budget and has its headquarters in New Delhi (source: Wikipedia) by an act of Parliament.

   Before 1981, the security of the PM was the responsibility of the Delhi police. In October 1981, a special task force (STF) was raised by the IB to provide ring-round and escort to the PM in and out of India. After the assassination of Indira Gandhi, the then PM of India, in October 1984, a special group was formed which was later renamed the SPG in March 1985 and came into being in April 1985.

   After the assassination of Rajiv Gandhi, in May 1991, the SPG Act was amended to provide security to former PMs for a period of ten years, but on November 2019, an SPG Amendment Bill asked to reduce the SPG cover only to the PM and his/her immediate kin and ex-PMs and family for five years.

2. Z-plus security has security of 55 personnel, including national security guards (NSG).

3. Z category has the cover of 22 personnel, including 4-5 NSG commandos.

4. Y category has a security cover of 11 persons, including one or two commandos

5. X category has security cover of 2 personnel, that is, two armed policemen.

In some cases, politicians make use of their category as a status symbol and may use their clout to secure Z or Z-plus category. This is often under criticism by the media and the public as a waste of taxpayer's money. Though some of them were phased out either from security cover or by lowering the category, controversies continue as many politicians remained under the Z-plus category and bureaucrats in the Y category.

Security failures:

Other important assassinations or attempts were as follows:

- John F Kennedy, former president of the US, November 1963

- the assassination of the King of Nepal and his entire family by the Crown prince

- Anwar Sadat, former president of Egypt, while receiving the salute of his own army parade

- Maimoon Adbul Khayoom, President of the Maldives

- Pervez Musharraf, president of Pakistan, on July 6, 2007, and December 25, 2003

- George W Bush, former president of the US, on May 10, 2006, and February 7, 2001.

- Sheikh Haseena, PM of Bangladesh, August 21, 2004

- Chen Shui Bian, ex-President of the Republic of China, on March 19, 2004

- Jacques Chirac, ex-President of France. July 14, 2002

- Chandrika Kumaratunga, President of Sri Lanka, on December 18, 1999.

- Muammar Gaddafi, Libyan leader, February 9, 1998

- Edward Shevardnadze, President, Georgia. February 9, 1998.

- Housni Mubarak, President Egypt, June 25, 1994

- Bill Clinton, ex-President of the US, October 29, 1994

- John Major, ex-PM of the UK, February 7, 1991

- Rajiv Gandhi, PM of India July 30, 1987

- Margaret Thatcher, ex-PM of the UK, October 12, 1984

- Pope John Paul II, May 12, 1982 and March 30, 1981

- Ronald Reagan, President of the US, March 13, 1981

- Richard Nixon, President of the US, February 17, 1974

Though the cause of death of former prime minister of India Lal Bahadur Shastri on January 11, 1966, at Tashkent, Uzbekistan, was reportedly cardiac arrest, even today, some people believe that there was something more to his death than the news that made its way back to his country. The possibility of the involvement of some dark forces cannot be ruled out. The Indo-Pak War of 1965 ended formally with the signing of the Tashkent Agreement on January 10, 1966, and he died the next day in Tashkent itself. The cause of death was in dispute and his family was not satisfied with the proffered explanation.

In modern times, political assassinations continue to play an important role in the political and social process. Many argue that the assassination of Israeli prime minister Yitzhak Rabin in 1985 was a major reason for the collapse of the process of peace talks between Israel and Palestine.

The importance of the assassinations of Martin Luther King, Jr., in the US and Benazir Bhutto of Pakistan have indeed changed the political scenarios in both countries.

The role of intelligence agencies

Intelligence agencies all over the world, including India, have a definite agenda of both prevention and execution. It is a known fact that the CIA, the KGB, Mossad and others have a history of assassination as well as protection of their respective leaders. Though the CIA has succeeded in executing its killing agenda, there were failed reported attempts to assassinate Fidel Castro of Cuba and Kim Jong Un, the supreme leader of North Korea.

All these incidents that were discussed in this chapter bring forth the many perils that always surround the leader of the country. He is elected by his people, but while in office, he is surrounded by wolves.

All this behoves the nation to provide him at his disposal the absolute power of knowledge of everything that goes around him.

THE FORCE ON THE GROUND INTEGRITY, DISCIPLINE AND OTHER PEOPLE CHALLENGES OF THE IOs AND THE POLICE

EIGHTEEN

CORRUPTION AND NEPOTISM

Corruption could be defined in simple terms as dishonest or fraudulent conduct by those in power or authority. In general, corruption is what prompts an action or inaction that amounts to abuse of power by people in authority, driven by dishonesty or criminal intent, in return for personal illicit gains

The Corruption Perception Index (CPI) published each year by Transparency International, ranks countries by their perceived levels of corruption as determined by expert assessment and surveys. India was 78th out of 175 countries as per the 2018 report. The least corrupt countries in the 2018 report were Denmark and New Zealand.

Corruption exists in intelligence agencies like the IB, RAW, CBI, Central Police Organisations (CPOs), state intelligence and state police in India; the FBI and CIA in the US, the KGB in Russia, the Chinese Intelligence Agency and the Pakistan Intelligence Bureau. Every intelligence and security agency in the world has dark secrets. Yet few know of the intense level of corruption, deception and nepotism in these agencies.

In mid-2019, newspapers flashed the news about the CBI booking its own Special Director for accepting Rs 2 crore from Mr. Moin Quereshi, a meat exporter, to sabotage a probe against Mr. Moin, and also RAW's second-in-command for colluding with him. This is probably just the tip of the iceberg, as corruption has become an accepted way of life among government employees particularly higher in the hierarchy. As many of these highly placed bureaucrats and police officers have political patronage, the culprits are seldom punished in a court of law. It is a paradox that in these cases the prosecuting agency itself is the culprit.

At times, reports emerge indicating that corruption has crept into the IB as well, particularly in the senior hierarchy. It is interesting to note that, as in the case of various intelligence agencies in other countries, the IB also has only limited accountability by virtue of the secret nature of its functioning. Hence, while people of integrity are respected in the department, for obvious reasons, others are found to be making extra money.

Nepotism seems to be on the increase in the bureau. Nepotism is similar to favouritism, where those with power or influence favour relatives or friends, especially by giving them untimely promotions, good postings and professional benefits. This leads to sycophancy or, in Hindi, *'chamchagiri'*. In other words, the honest and efficient officers are at times side-lined and promotions and other fringe benefits denied them. This leads to further disgruntlement and frustration among the middle- and lower-cadre officers. Undoubtedly, such a state of affairs decreases the overall efficiency of intelligence collection.

There are double agents who work both for the recruiting country and the enemy country, either out of fear or out of pecuniary considerations. It is known that some RAW officers posted in the US and other countries escaped and never returned to India.

One double agent was a senior RAW officer during the time of the LTTE operations in Sri Lanka, who was passing information to the American CIA. He was reportedly seen by a junior intelligence officer coming out of a five-star hotel in Chennai with a foreign woman. The officer reported the matter to his immediate boss in Chennai, who is said to have scolded the junior officer and ignored the report at that time. But later, when army personnel dropped from a helicopter in Sri Lanka were gunned down by the LTTE, the helicopter pilot returned and reported to his superiors that information must have been leaked. This created utter confusion and anxiety among senior officers of the RAW and the IB, who then searched for any earlier reports that could shed light on the possible leakage of information that was known only to five top officials of the security agencies and defence. Then the report about the RAW officer submitted by the junior IO a few months before was brought out and sent to IB headquarters.

Ultimately, the officer was asked to come to Delhi supposedly on some official work, but he was whisked away from the aircraft by IB sleuths immediately after landing in Delhi. On interrogation, the officer revealed that he was passing information to the CIA agent for wine, women and wealth. Nevertheless, the officer was not prosecuted but dismissed from service. Later it was heard that the officer and his family members were placed somewhere in the US.

Similarly, another senior officer at IB headquarters, who was very close to the high echelons in Delhi and who was considered a very brilliant and resourceful person, was also caught spying for the CIA for money and wine. Interestingly, in this case, the officer was found driving his own car around the Diplomatic Enclave, which normally doesn't happen as every senior officer is given cars and drivers by the department. A surveillance team in the diplomatic areas of New Delhi reported the matter to the higher-ups, as a result of which the officer was questioned first by an interrogation team and then by the Director himself. The Director instructed the accused officer to take voluntary retirement in order to avoid embarrassment to the department. Interestingly, he also seems to be in the US at present, as if the CIA is highly benevolent in helping its spies anywhere in the world.

As per an excellent article in the Indian Express titled 'Beware of corruption in post-COVID times', by ex-Kerala Chief Secretary Mr K. Jayakumar:

Embedded as it is in the climate of self-reliance and an undeclared trade war with China, trends of accelerated economic development and investment promotion are clearly foreboding. Ensuring ease of doing business should not sound the death knell for the necessary checks and balances in a system. This misplaced enthusiasm, among other collateral damages, has the potential to create a dangerous tolerance towards corruption, one of the most cancerous maladies of our polity and society. Strangely, corruption, though ubiquitous across the country, is the least discussed malady in political and administrative circles. But that complacency will prove to be quite costly as the nation embarks on the path of a new self-reliant economic miracle.

Corruption: International check-posts

History of Corruption at Airports: Before the formation of the Bureau of Immigration (BoI), immigration all over India was looked after by the respective state police. The Foreigners Regional Registration Officer (FRRO) is appointed in each state by the state police and the FRRO is normally an officer of the rank of SP or Deputy Commissioner of Police. A check on foreigners is required mainly at airports, seaports and border check-posts. It was observed that the state police were not managing this department properly and had started taking bribes, thereby compromising national security at various checkpoints. This ultimately led the government to form the BoI as a special arm of the IB. A joint Director Rank officer of the IB was to head the BoI from New Delhi.

Though the IB was entrusted with this responsibility in the early 1970s, all the states, with the exception of Tamil Nadu, continued to manage this new organisation with existing police officials, by deputing officers to the IB and drawing their pay from the IB itself. This system was found to be nothing but a follow-up of the earlier state policing. The IB initially allowed these deputations with the rationale that since Immigration officers dealt with the general public, there could be possibilities of arguments and counterarguments, followed by taking certain passengers into custody, which were basically police functions.

The practice of police officers managing immigration earlier had resulted in security lapses, and there were incidents of unwanted and anti-national elements entering and exiting India. There was a furore in Parliament about these lacunae, which ultimately had prompted the IB to take over the entire immigration aspect.

However, the system of dual functioning of the FRRO both in the IB as well as in the State Special Branch even now continues in certain states. When IB officers were inducted into the BoI, the police officers who were already in the immigration department simply continued into these new roles under new clothing.

It is undeniable that before the IB stepped in there was an organised system of corruption in these airports, ever since the Gulf opened up for employment in the 1960s. Many skilled and unskilled workers started flowing to Gulf countries, mainly for the construction work there. These workers had not even matriculated and women went to the Gulf mostly for odd jobs like housemaids, *aayahs* and sweepers. Reports emerged of these workers suffering from difficulties and torture and under inhuman conditions at the work site. The Government of India then decided to check the outflow of workers by establishing a department known as Protector of Emigrants (PoE) under the Ministry of Labour. Accordingly, the Labour Ministry appointed an officer at the joint secretary level as Chief of Protectorate of Emigrants and PoE officers in various states.

According to PoE instructions, every employee or worker who was not a graduate going to the Gulf and a few other countries was required to get PoE clearance before departure. Such workers were normally recruited by recruiting agents. (All recruiting agents were to be registered with PoE.) These instructions created further breeding grounds for corruption.

Between the 1960s and 1980s, it was said that to get postings as a PoE, one had to shell out a huge amount (say Rs 50 lakh to Rs 1 crore) to their head in Delhi and the Ministry of Labour. The recruiting agents collected the bribe amount along with the normal approved fees from the candidates that are paid regularly to the PoE. At immigration in the airport, nobody was supposed to be sent to the countries mentioned above without a PoE clearance certificate on their passport. However, the immigration officials in the Gulf countries were not bothered about the PoE clearance but only looked at the visa. This made the PoE clearance almost unattainable using the normal route. It would not be surprising to know that an average of 500 such workers boarded planes from Mumbai every day.

It was against this backdrop that the government decided to finally step in and sanitise things. The role of the PoE was drastically diluted by lifting the restrictions on qualifications of workers bound for the Gulf and other countries.

Eventually, the Protectorate of Emigrants relaxed its rules by which diploma holders, nurses and others were excluded from employment clearance checks. Though custom officials have loopholes to circumvent the situation and were still getting bribes, the quantum of the malpractice has considerably decreased. It is now understood that a posting at Immigration is no more a prize or a lucrative posting, thanks to the sincere countermeasures and strict actions taken by a few senior officers in the IB.

Talking about non-IB departments at international checkpoints, it is worth mentioning here that the maximum corruption at that time was prevalent among the customs officers at airports and seaports, and the accumulation of illicit money was on an unimaginable scale. In addition to the money, they collected foreign goods such as liquor bottles, cigarettes, electronic goods and clothes from the incoming passengers. This was nothing but extortion and looting.

This practice went on till early 2010. Following complaints from various quarters and from some family members of the customs officials themselves (as the flow of unearned money led many customs officials to become addicted to drinks, women and gambling, which ultimately spoiled family life) and also new security threats, CCTVs were installed. This one piece of technological made revolutionary changes in the corruption scenario at the airports.

Nevertheless, the fact remains that customs, Central Excise and Income Tax are still generally perceived to be the most corrupt departments. In short, every revenue-earning department is notorious for corruption. According to the findings of Local Circles and Transparency International India (LCTII), published in November 2019, bribery appeared to decline in 2018, but increased during 2019. More than 50 percent of Indians bribed government officials in 2019, with Rajasthan in the number one position, where seven out of ten people paid bribes. Most bribes were paid for property registrations followed by bribes to the police, municipal corporations, transport offices, tax departments, water departments, electricity boards and others in states. In the Central Government departments, corruption continues nowadays, but at a low pace. According to the survey, which was conducted in 20 states in India, the respondents said that bribery was the only way to ensure that government officials would complete their work and that no serious action has been taken to curb corruption. This tendency existed even before Independence, and it has led the majority of people to think that moderate and benevolent corruption is acceptable and only the real crooks and greedy should be dealt with. They also ask how the system could be corrected if the anti-corruption department in states and the CBI at the Centre themselves are corrupt.

Another interesting example is an incident in which a senior police officer came on deputation to the IB and was heading the IB unit in a state. When he was offered a higher post in the State Police, he went back to the state cadre and superannuated from there. However, immediately after his retirement from government service, he was offered a high-level post in a charitable trust. This trust was floated by a multinational company with its Indian promoters who were involved in an infamous defence equipment scam which was then under investigation by the CBI. A top-level person in the multinational company gave a middle-level IB officer a tip that the police officer had been inducted into the trust to get his assistance to obtain advance information on the day-to-day CBI moves in this scam. Besides an attractive salary and allowance, the multinational company bore all travel and other expenditures for the officer. His frequent visits to Delhi to influence his juniors in the CBI circle investigating the scam and also to know the day-to-day developments was clear evidence of the ultimate intention of the MNC. Though the report was submitted by the middle-level officer to his bosses, whether it was taken to a logical endpoint is unknown.

A few directly recruited middle-level officers were also found to be involved in corrupt practices, but the majority of them were shielded by their guardian angels higher up in the hierarchy. The infamous Purulia arms and ammunitions drop incident continues to be in the minds of the general public. A private plane carrying arms and ammunition in large quantities landed at Varanasi airport for refuelling. Interestingly, the Air Traffic Control (ATC) at Varanasi airport neither raised an objection nor attempted to intercept the flight. When the plane continued its flight from Varanasi, an Air Force station noticed the flight and immediately passed the information to on their headquarters in Delhi, which instructed the Air Force to intercept the unauthorised flight. Two fighter planes intercepted the plane and instructed the pilot of the flight to land at a nearby airport. The information was also passed on to the IB in the state in the middle of the night and the Deputy Director, SIB, conveyed the message to the Security Control Staff of the IB posted at the domestic airport. The plane was forcibly made to land at the nearby airport and the police personnel posted at the airport security in the airport area surrounded the aircraft parked at a dark place in the airport.

Kim Davy, a Denmark national who was the leader of the arms drop operation, came out of the aircraft and walked to the terminal building without any objection from either the security police or the airport staff. Kim Davy came directly to the exit gate, where he was blocked by an IB officer as the latter had information about the incident. To everybody's surprise, Kim Davy was allowed to leave for unknown reasons. The main culprit vanished from the area and is still at large while others in the aircraft were arrested and prosecuted in accordance with Indian law. It remains a mystery why the IB officer allowed Kim Davy to exit. When senior officers arrived at the spot and enquired about the whole episode, the IB officer on duty expressed his ignorance about the white man who was the main suspect. No one knows what transpired between them that day. Is it to be assumed that Kim Davy succeeded in getting the better of the department by a timely act, a smooth operation with a vulnerable IO that day? No further enquiry in this regard took place afterwards.

Several similar cases of corruption, dishonesty and doubtful integrity of a few officers still continue to go unquestioned. There could be a large number of such cases. That is why it has been reiterated that a separate cadre, such as the IIS or ISS should be introduced with a view to ensuring that people of high integrity and efficiency can continue in the IB.

NINETEEN

DISCIPLINE IN POLICE AND INTELLIGENCE ORGANISATIONS

By convention, discipline requires enforcement; seldom is it cultivated. The Indian police forces, including intelligence organisations, modelling themselves on the pattern and structure of the armed forces and governed by the archaic tenets enacted 140 years ago, has ever turned a blind eye to the sweeping currents of changes in the concept and practice of modern management of organisations. As a result, the formidable police force and intelligence system is weakened as an organisation; the rot has already set in, manifesting itself in the declining standard of discipline for which it had once been renowned. It is only symptomatic of a malignant disease growing within; the sooner it is diagnosed, the greater are the chances of cure.

The modern man, sensitive to the changes everywhere, would refuse to equate himself with a machine; neither will he accept an assault on his self-respect. He can be motivated to do things not by what Follett calls "the power over" but by "the power with. Instruction from the top down is fast being replaced by suggestions from the bottom up and the role of management is more that of a coordinator and facilitator than of a controller and director. The synergy generated from teamwork moves mountains. Resentment of authority is basic to human nature and pervades society, in which the police force and intelligence organisations also exist.

People are motivated to do things by an inborn desire to be an achiever and an actualiser of self-set goals. Abraham Maslow's hierarchy of human needs, one of the basic concepts of worker motivation, delineates five types of human needs that prompt people to do things in the order in which each need is satisfied—physical needs, safety and security needs, social needs, ego and esteem needs and self-actualisation needs.

Indiscipline is on the increase, exemplified by the growing instances of cases for disciplinary proceedings, a general lack of involvement and commitment among the rank and file, rampant corruption, disinterest and insecurity among the workforce, the general state of inefficiency and cynicism and the strongly felt need for greater unionisation. We might first explore the causes instead of analysing the effects.

Trade unionism in some form or the other does exist in many state forces, both at the top and at the lower ranks. The efforts of certain directly recruited IB officers to vent their grievances through an association during the Janata Party regime immediately after the 1977 elections was, however, later suppressed and the leaders of such movement were either suppressed or dismissed from the service under Article 311 2c of the Constitution, which gives the government the power to dismiss any of its employees without a trial in a court of law for anti-national and security reasons.

The police force, though it wields power, is treated at a discount for any ambitious man aiming to advance his career. The methods of selection are also handicapped owing to the low demand from the more desirable candidates in the job market. Society tries to keep the police force at an arm's distance if given an option. The dividing chasm between the police and civilians results in a feeling of alienation, which, if given a choice, a policeman would like to avoid. There is compartmentalisation and a hierarchical discrimination. The executive layers cater more to developing servitude than camaraderie. The policeman comes into the force with ambitions, but is invariably forced to toe the line and follow instructions, to follow protocols and routines in the case-files that he handles, protocols mostly designed to benefit the bureaucracy and its political affiliations rather than enabling the liberty of analytical thought and curiosity.

Though the IB is not accepted as a police organisation, many of the top posts are occupied by police officers from the state police and most of them go back to their own states about 5 or 10 years after deputation, as a result of which, many secrets and methods of operation of the IB are compromised and the directly recruited officers in the IB who are the pillars of the department are not taken care of. A new recruit who has studiously researched and decided to avoid the police force in favour of intelligence work joins the IB, only to find himself placed underneath an administrative layer comprising police officers deputed from the states.

A closer look at the malaise reveals far too many snags in the system that has allowed indiscipline to spawn. Basically, it has failed to satisfy the needs of the workforce outlined in Maslow's hierarchy. Having failed to motivate the force and cultivate discipline in a congenial climate, complaining about the fall of the standards of discipline appears a pitiable exercise in futility. It is high time that we realise that a sense of discipline should be felt within that is reflected in performance. The concept of a 'whipped-up' discipline has already been eschewed by society at large and is as dead as a dodo except perhaps in the police force.

Let us begin with the basic physical needs of the workforce, the provision of which lead to a feeling of being cared for by the organisation. The theory that should govern the settlement of wages and the availing of perquisites is that compensation should have a direct relationship with the nature of the job, the risk involved, the working conditions, task completion time, the competence and the ability of the employee, the degree of responsibility and the extent of power and the status in society.

Moving on to security needs, policemen, who are the custodians of law and order, and intelligence officers helping the police, who deal with law breakers and anti-social elements to protect law-abiding citizens, are ever exposed to high-risk working conditions; the vulnerability being greater at the frontlines than at state or central headquarters. They have no fixed working hours. But in terms of pay and perquisites, they are treated at par with any other government servants on grades equal to the ranks. They are also denied the right to protest and make legitimate demands through organised forums. Instead they are kept at the mercy of the government, which is seldom merciful and generous to those who are unorganised.

The sense of insecurity pervading the organisation has two aspects: the insecurity for the physical self and that for the vocation. The Indian police force is adequately equipped only to meet the threats of unarmed opponents. In these days of sophisticated weaponry smuggled in to arm opponents, our constabulary is left with an arsenal left over from the British Era and bamboo lathis. Their training is also inadequate to meet the challenges facing the protectors of law and order.

As a result, the police withdraw meekly in situations that pose a threat to their security; they are often on the defensive rather than on the offensive. Human resources being the prime source of power for the police force, streamlining the training programme with periodic refresher courses, arming the forces to meet the needs of the various anticipated situations and granting them a certain amount of freedom and discretion to wield power and use justifiable force as necessary will instil confidence in their minds and prop up their sagging spirits.

As far as IB recruits are concerned, the training is far better than that for the normal police force in helping them cope with day-to-day situations.

Honest police and intelligence officers often fall prey to the intrigue of coteries of vested interests in and outside the organisations and are often made scapegoats, creating instances for many others to toe the line of groups with nefarious interests.

In order to counter the growing discontent among the police and intelligence officials and the exposure of the media, a few commissions were appointed, such as the Police Commission for police reforms and the Shankaran Nair Commission for IB recruits, but their findings were seldom implemented. As a result, the people who are in the field continue to be disgruntled and dissatisfied with their career prospects and perks in proportion to the risks involved in their field work.

It is interesting to note at this juncture that the late Arun Nehru, who was the Minister of State for internal security during the Rajiv Gandhi era, himself volunteered to be with a surveillance team of the IB in Delhi. Having realised the risks and difficulties involved in field work, he sanctioned a huge sum of money for field officers of the IB, but the deserving lot received only peanuts.

As the family is the immediate first circle of society for an individual, measures for the comfort and wellbeing of an employee's family should be the prime consideration when meeting the employee's social needs. Cross-country transfers in the IB, which result in the dislocation in the employee's establishment, should be minimised and the hardships of such moves mitigated by initiating a series of staff welfare and facilitation measures. There are absolutely no rules for transfers and promotions in the department. Things move according to the wisdom, or, sometimes, the whims and fancies, of the senior bosses.

Status in society comes next in Maslow's hierarchy. A well-planned strategy needs to be chalked out to dispel the perception of the public of the police and intelligence forces as oppressors and part of an ostracised section of society.

Ego needs are individual-specific and are difficult to generalise. However, the basics remain the craving for recognition as an achiever and appreciation for the effort put in. Years of experience have proven that the carrot pays better than the stick. A scientifically stipulated intensive system brings more benefits than the timeworn system of reprimand and chastisement in the name of discipline and secrecy.

When custom and enforcement officials earn fabulous incentives, as a matter of fact, many of their achievements are based on the inputs given either by the police or the IB. The argument is that customs, excise, income tax and such departments are revenue-earning and a portion of the revenue is shared with them. Think of a situation where there is lawlessness and chaos and the very security of the country is compromised. In such a situation, revenue-earning departments become useless. It is to be mentioned here that highly educated young people join the IB as direct recruits with great ambition and aspiration. Later, they find themselves underpaid and humiliated at the hands of those who do not belong to the department but are outsiders, who come for a short period from the state police. The long-pending demand for creating an Indian Intelligence service like any other civil service is yet to be fulfilled, though RAW, the external spy agency introduced the Research & Analysis Service (R & AS) for direct recruits.

TWENTY

HEROES ARE HUMAN TOO

The personal difficulties and needs of an intelligence officer

Hence it is that with none in the whole army are more intimate relations to be maintained than with spies.

– Sun Tzu, The Art of War, XIII, 14

IOs are usually the most under-appreciated and ignored lot, but they are a highly important set of people working for national security. Not many are known, because their exploits are classified and not for public consumption. The case of the National Security Advisor, Shri Ajit Doval, whose adventures and high-risk operations are now known to the public, is a rarity. Though he is from the state cadre of Kerala, he joined the IB at an early age by virtue of his spirit of adventure and thirst for spy work. His interest in intelligence work made him continue in the department till he ascended to its top position. It was a rare case in which the IPS officers coming on deputation to the IB were involved directly in the field operations, taking great risks to collect hard intelligence.

It is in the public domain that he spent nearly seven years infiltrating into Pakistani territory undercover and provided very useful information. While posted in Northeast India, where insurgency was at its peak, Shri Doval proved his mettle by befriending the insurgents and ultimately cracking them. He walked deep into China to negotiate with the Mizoram Liberation Army chief, which ultimately made the insurgents come to the negotiating table and led to the end of insurgency.

Shri Rameshwar Nath Kao (R N Kao), who was said to have been photographed only twice in his career, was responsible for the creation of RAW by virtue of his close association with the then Prime Minister Smt. Indira Gandhi. His life has been always inconspicuous, like that of a true intelligence officer.

The story of Ravindra Kaushik, who allegedly infiltrated into the Pakistan Army under deep cover, is known to the public now. He learnt Urdu and was circumcised. He married a Pakistani girl, managed to get into the Pakistan Army and became a major. He passed valuable information but was later caught by the Pakistanis and tortured for about two years before being given a death sentence.

Kashmir Singh spent 35 years in Pakistan undertaking espionage activities but was caught by the ISI in Pakistan. It is said that he was chained to a post in a cell and did not see daylight for over 17 years. He became insane and was pardoned by Pakistani political leadership on humanitarian grounds and returned to India in 2008.

There are various stories of espionage and sufferings. It is to be understood that an intelligence officer who is sent to an enemy country has to undergo a lot of tension, agony and even punishment for his failure.

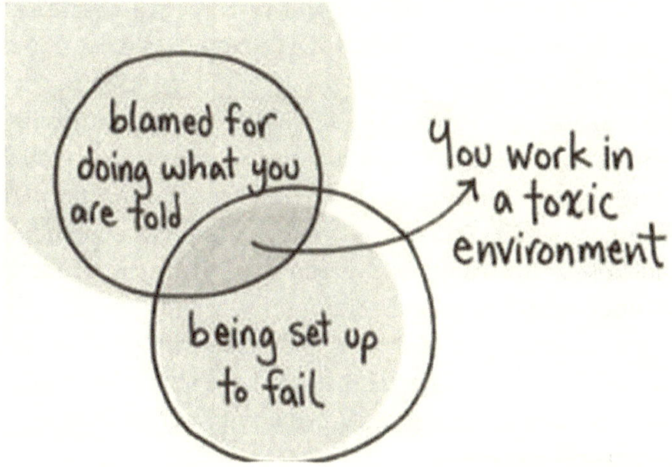

In January 2018, an Indian intelligence officer allegedly infiltrated an Islamic State ring to track and arrest an Afghan bomber sent to hit Delhi. The operation is said to have included the Indian 'plant' supplying the operation with explosives without triggers and he even arranged accommodation for the bomber in Delhi. This bomber was an operative who lived in New Delhi in the guise of an engineering student. He was caught and flown to custody in Afghanistan after his arrest in Delhi for interrogation by key US and Afghan military and intelligence officers. Though he was arrested in September 2017, the news was disclosed only in June 2018. His confession and interrogations were among the possible reasons behind the success of US forces against the Taliban in Afghanistan.

All such good work by the IOs barely ever makes out of the shadows, which was where it was executed in the first place. This is not incorrect. There is no doubt that maintaining the secrecy of such operations is paramount for the department and personnel involved.

Such struggles in silence, and in perpetual obscurity, without one's successes ever being acknowledged, let alone celebrated, comes as part of the IO's job. Bhisma in the Puranas and Sun Tzu in 'The Art of War' have categorically called out for special attention to the grievances of the King's spies. While Bhisma stresses on ensuring proper remuneration, Sun Tzu talks of keeping them contented and close at hand since the direction of alignment of their loyalties single-handedly determines victory or failure of the enterprise. Loyalties could motivate someone to embark on the path of a doomed spy or, on the other hand, be lured by the enemy into becoming a converted spy, working on his behalf.

The question to ask is to what extent is the humanness of our spies, our IOs taken into account by the department? Does there even exist a departmental function for people issues and grievance redressal?

Abraham Maslow's 1943 paper "A Theory of Human Motivation" provides a highly popular hierarchical representation of human needs, something that has been used as a reference framework during sociology research for decades.

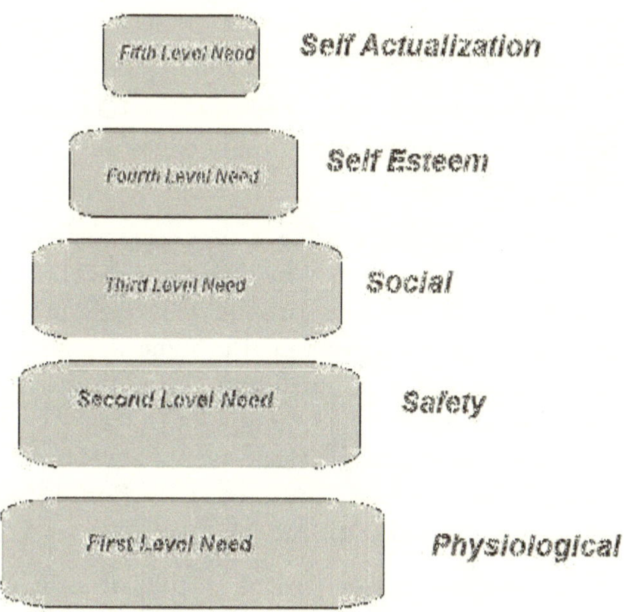

The paper argues that there are five hierarchical levels in the need structure of human beings. The very first level is the most primal needs, the physiological needs, which include food and water, health, sleep, clothes and shelter. Safety needs refer primarily to personal and financial security, but also includes the availability of healthcare and protection of one's general well-being.

Once these two levels of needs are met, a human being desires social belonging and inclusion. This leads to the next level of needs, for social status and other ego needs. Self-esteem is something closely tied to social recognition, appreciation, importance and most importantly respect from peers and society. All this cultivates within a person a sense of freedom, capability, competence, self-confidence, mastery, and pride. Self-actualisation is a perceived want for 'becoming', for fulfilling one's destiny and realising one's full potential.

All these needs being met feeds into an IO's motivation and hence increases his positive energies: his credibility, integrity and efficiency.

The IO, the human, achieves the greatest sense of pride and self-actualisation when he feels that the risks he took mattered, and that the information he brought in was put to use to make his country safer in some way. Of course, the decision to use the intelligence should rest with the government, but it would mean a lot to the foot soldier, who lives and dies in the shadows, playing shadow wars with the nation's enemies, to feel that his efforts have been instrumental in aiding the nation's cause.

He is not a private agent, a paid assassin or an unscrupulous agent who has no emotional connection to the cause and only executes the job in return for the money he gets paid. Rather, he sees himself has a phantom warrior for the country. This passion should be nurtured even further.

It is true that too much passion and emotion can blur a person's vision, but the power of passion shouldn't be underestimated at all, especially when most of the enemies he is fighting with are primarily driven by pure passion and extremism. True, the IO should not be impulsive, but at the same time should not act indifferent or purely from routine either.

Avner Kaufman, the leader of the hit team for Mossad's Operation Wrath of God, the organised assassination of individual sponsors of the Black September terrorist group as vengeance for the 1972 massacre of the Israeli

Olympians, used to have nightmares about the killings of his countrymen that kept him awake at night, and this continued through the operation.

In October 1972, Kaufman and his wife had watched in horror as the TV coverage showed the terrorists blowing up the two helicopters filled with Israeli hostages. The horrific scenes of the massacre had stayed with him and fuelled his resolve and perseverance while he and his team took down their Black September targets one by one.

Yes, an IO, our shadow warrior, fuelled by true grit, will go miles further in his mission as compared to one that doesn't have his heart in the cause. This will be possible when he achieves all the levels of his human needs, and when he attributes his self-actualisation to his department and his nation.

A supportive work culture and a healthy work environment are things that should be absolutely taken for granted for an IO, considering that he is already under a great deal of stress. Perhaps a clock has been ticking away that only he understands, and he has been running against time trying to achieve near-impossible targets.

The fact that he is committed to secrecy means he cannot divulge details of the challenges he is facing. He cannot open up in front of a psychiatrist like police personnel are encouraged to do nowadays. He cannot share any of this with his family; there is a constant distance that forms between him and his family as he remains cocooned away from them physically and emotionally. And imagine the mental turmoil he has to go through because he 'knows things', truths, probably some that are explosive in nature. The burden of being the keeper of the nation's secrets might become too much to bear.

He cannot even turn to the spies shown on celluloid and pretend that they are depicting him, that someone is telling his story, as the spy shown in the movies doesn't look one bit like him. The gadgets they use look unreal and their social life and hobbies are mostly about things he never even knew existed.

After all this, the last thing he needs is to get tangled up in the bureaucracies of his own department. As in any other institution, confusion and misaligned priorities among the administrative layer and the ground force are the main challenges an IO faces in office.

An intelligence officer seems very powerful but, in reality, he or she has no executive powers given by the enactment of any law by the Indian Parliament. The IB exists on paper but has no statutory base. Once a person joins the IB, he or she has to forget all the glamour associated with other civil servants. An IO will hardly get any media attention. He or she has to serve the country day and night more than anyone else, but what he or she will get in return is absolutely nothing except the mental satisfaction of achievement. Those who go after power, fame and money normally betray the country. The life of an IO, in short, is very difficult and thankless and the IO has to sacrifice or compromise with his or her family life.

After passing an All India written examination and interview followed by a medical test, middle officers in the IB have to undergo different types of training—physical, mental, in weaponry—at various centres in India, to make their minds and bodies strong enough to react to a situation in the best possible way. An IO has to maintain high values of honesty and integrity. Till 1975, the minimum academic qualification to join the middle cadre was a first-class graduation or second-class post-graduation. This requirement was later relaxed to graduation, which is the basic qualification for any all-India service examination like the IAS, IPS and allied services conducted by the UPSC. As mentioned earlier, all the senior posts in the IB are occupied by police officers on deputation from state cadres. In most cases, these go back to their states, as many cannot easily adjust to intelligence work. Unfortunately, there is no workable grievance cell in the department and many field officers who joined the department with great expectations and aspirations for career prospects are disillusioned and at times frustrated. In spite of all these lacunae, the IB continues to work with efficiency in the security scenario and is always appreciated by the ruling government and other departments.

We often sing songs about our valiant and brave army and uniformed police personnel, as they rightly deserve appreciation and encouragement because of their sacrifices for the country. But seldom do we give a thought to the invisible knights who work in the shadows unnamed and unknown, and ultimately fade back into obscurity like ghostly apparitions. How many spies give crucial information that leads to successful operations and victories by defence and police forces? How many died without a 21-gun salute and state honours, without having received a medal openly at the Republic Day parade or in any public function? How many silently do their jobs behind enemy lines, where they could be caught the next second and tortured for years? But they continue to do their jobs without grumbling, doubts or rewards.

TWENTY-ONE

SUGGESTIONS AND COMMENTS

Overall revamping is urgently required in all intelligence and police organisations in the country to make them more efficient and people-friendly. A new sense of confidence should be brought in among the police and intelligence forces by introducing necessary reforms. For this, passing acts in Parliament and State Assemblies is required. The age-old and obsolete traditions and practices that prevailed in the police and police-controlled intelligence setup have to be given up. Rewriting the old and primitive interpersonal relations within the system, particularly in senior–junior hierarchy, seems to be the need of the day. The British culture of imposing impractical orders on subordinates without providing for their basic needs while the senior officials are sitting comfortably should immediately be stopped to create confidence, vigour and vitality among the staff.

The modern system of management propounded by Abraham Maslow known as the Maslovian Theory of Management, explained earlier in this book could be followed. Youngsters who are highly qualified join the intelligence organisation aspiring to great things, but they are deprived of basic things: timely promotions, postings and fringe benefits. This leads to frustration and disgruntlement amongst the executive officers, which, in turn, affect the overall efficiency of intelligence output.

Human beings want not to become rich but to become richer. Directly recruited officers, who are mostly postgraduates, join the departments in the middle cadre as ACIO Grade II, and normally retire as Assistant Directors with three promotions. Interestingly, the majority of the supporting staff, who are not entrusted with intelligence collection, are generally given four promotions and sometimes more. In practice, it is the supporting staff who decide the promotions and postings of executive officers as the senior officer in charge normally agrees with what the supporting staff put up to him, unless he has a personal interest in certain cases.

In effect, the IB is neither a police organisation nor a civil department. For certain things, the IB is compared with central police organisations for the award of Indian Police Medals (IPM) while for all other aspects it is considered a civil organisation. While CPOs are given various benefits, such as quick promotions and extra allowances, IB executive officers are denied such benefits on the interpretation that the IB is not a police organisation.

During its formation and ever since, in order to fill up various vacancies, several personnel from the state police were inducted into the IB on deputation and police officers have become both the de facto and de jure controllers of the IB and all its covert and overt activities.

The immediate need of the day is to introduce a separate cadre service in the IB such as the Indian Intelligence Service (IIS) or Indian Security Service (ISS) as in the case of RAW, where the day an executive officer is promoted to the Class I Gazetted Rank, he or she is conferred with R & AS. In the revenue department of the government of India, as soon as any officer becomes Class I, Indian Revenue Service (IRS) is conferred. This is a major discrimination against the IB.

There is no proper grievance cell in the IB to address the genuine grievances of the employees. The formation of an association or union and even mass petitions are prohibited in the department. In the late 1970s, the attempt by a few directly recruited executive officers to form an association was shattered, resulting in the dismissal of three such officers named Mr. Varghese Joseph, alias Joseph Kennedy, Mr. A. K. Kaul and Mr. B. B. Raval under Article 311 (C).

The introduction of a separate cadre for the IB would provide enthusiasm and the feeling of being at home. All deputation officers are to be repatriated to the state cadres after three to five years of deputation and only officers who are found to be fit for the IB should be absorbed. The deputation of inefficient and disinterested officers is in no way helpful to the IB but is only a burden as their allegiance is to their respective states.

TWENTY-TWO
IN CONCLUSION

India is probably the only country in the world where the heads of intelligence organisations are police officers on deputation from state cadres. These officers have the option of going back to their parent cadres even after serving in the IB for many years.

The national security threats that India confronts today are much more diverse and complex than ever before. These threats range from nuclear armed adversaries like China and Pakistan to Maoist elements, militancy, insurgency and Islamic terrorism arising from within its borders and beyond. The question that one must ask is whether the country has strategic measures to counter these challenges and the willingness and ability to confront them.

The tasks before India's intelligence community are similar to those that confront their counterparts across the world. These are related to strategic intelligence, anticipatory intelligence, current operations, cyber intelligence, counterterrorism, counter proliferation and counterintelligence. These subjects undoubtedly require integrated mission and enterprise management, as well as innovation. They are contingent upon the security challenges faced by a nation at a given time and necessitate reform and reorientation.

Historically, intelligence agencies have been forced to reform and restructure because of failures. A number of commissions have been appointed from time to time to reform and restructure intelligence agencies. Their reports highlight the lack of political will and departmental leadership guidance and examine why recommendations made by previous commissions and committees have not been implemented. The biggest problem has been the lack of coordination amongst the intelligence community in India. Each agency looks out for itself and guards its own interest. There is a need for strict guidance and supervision to ensure that there is cooperation and coordination.

After the 26/11 terrorist attack in Mumbai in 2008, the then Union Home Minister initiated the enforcement of coordination at the apex level, but subsequent Home Ministers have not kept up the process. There are currently 14 intelligence agencies operating in India with different and at times overlapping mandates. Most of these intelligence agencies came into being as a response to the changing strategic environments and shortcomings in the intelligence framework from time to time. For example, the directorate general of security (DGS) was formed within the IB after the 1962 war with China, with its operational unit the Aviation Research Centre (ARC) tasked with obtaining intelligence from China. Following the failure of the IB in providing information prior to the 1965 war against Pakistan, the government decided to hive off external intelligence under a new agency named the Research & Analysis Wing (RAW).

Though there were various measures of internal reorganisation and restructuring, the next wave of reforms came only after the 1999 Kargil War, when there was a colossal failure on the part of security agencies in detecting Pakistani incursions across the Line of Control (LOC). China's growth and the multiplication of its capabilities require a more focused effort in TECHINT (technical intelligence) and HUMINT (human intelligence). Accordingly, in 2004, the National Technical Research Organisation (NTRO) was set up to be the premier TECHINT agency of the country with a mandate to collect communications intelligence (COMINT), electronic intelligence (ELINT) and cyber intelligence. The creation of the NTRO created a storm as its mandates were already given to other intelligence services, including the IB, resulting in inter-agency turf battles that led to problems in its functioning for nearly a decade.

The question of accountability in the Indian context is no less important. Hardly anyone is held accountable for serious failures on the security front. This has led to a culture where no person or agency is held responsible for major intelligence failures and hence intelligence agencies have had little or no accountability. This is mainly due to the excessive secrecy with which intelligence organisations work. It is a systemic flaw; authority and accountability do not go together.

India's internal security environment is fraught with a number of challenges: cross-border terrorism, Maoist attacks, insurgencies in Northeast India, violent Islamic extremism, communal and sectarian violence, illegal migration, human trafficking, narcotics smuggling and money laundering. Such a wide gamut of threats requires a multi-pronged approach to intelligence gathering, which would be beyond the remit of a single agency.

As mentioned earlier, the Indian intelligence system emerged as an extension of the British police system to track and counter the Indian national movement. This is a legacy and structure that has not yet emerged to meet the challenges of modern intelligence gathering. It carries the burden of an intellectual infrastructure that has failed to build competencies essential to intelligence operations in a vastly different environment than the pre-Independence era. The lack of a dedicated intelligence cadre and the continuing practice of staffing intelligence agencies with police officers has resulted in downplaying the importance of language specialists, social scientists, technical specialists and cyber analysts. Over the years, the IB has become a reporting arm of the government, often treated as an appendage of the Ministry of Home Affairs (MHA). The tight political control by the MHA made the IB focus more on domestic and political matters at the expense of other security challenges. The agency also has responsibility over local police functions in the form of verifications and background checks, which further ties down its already limited manpower. All these factors put together have drastically compromised the IB's capabilities, especially in the areas of counterintelligence.

In 2001, a group of ministers (GoM) recommended an end to this practice and sought to confer the rank of Secretary to the Director of the IB on par with the status of the RAW counterpart. On the basis of this GoM advice, the IB was designated as the premier counterterrorism agency and authorised to create multi-agency centres (MAC) and subsidiary multi-agency centres (SMACs) to collate and process intelligence inputs from various sources. However, both MACs and SMACs in states so far have not taken any visible or fruitful steps.

First and foremost, the Indian government needs to decide what challenges must be addressed by its multiple intelligence agencies. It should decide what kind of an intelligence system would best serve internal and external security requirements and how best to strike a balance between traditional politico-military intelligence operations in target countries. Further, the question arises about how much emphasis should be laid on economic, commercial and scientific intelligence. In fact, a certain level of redundancy among intelligence agencies can prevent a systemic failure in one outfit from becoming a catastrophic and all-round failure.

Among democracies, India alone lacks any oversight of its intelligence agencies. Its agencies do not have any constitutional authority. The very existence of the IB is based on an executive order. It has no constitutional statute. Attempts have been made to move a private bill to regulate the status of the IB under an act passed in Parliament. In other countries, particularly in the US, a specific Parliamentary Committee monitors and scrutinises the finance, achievements, failures, grievances of personnel and administrative and operational matters. Every attempt to implement such a system in India has either been torpedoed by the government or the top echelons of the IB. The IB Director enjoys the status of a four-star general, besides being the topmost police officer of the country and Chairman of the Conference of Directors General of Police. The present system of the IB has continued from time immemorial and it seems that nobody wants to make any change, for unknown reasons. The IB has had to cut a sorry figure on many occasions that challenged its own existence from different quarters, but successfully managed to circumvent every situation in the name of secrecy. Even the ministers at the top level, including the Prime Minister, seem to be reluctant to antagonise the IB bosses in the complex and unstable political scenario that has existed since Independence.

One of the major problems with the IB is the challenge of addressing personnel issues. These include personnel shortages arising from the inability to recruit the right kind of people for specific tasks. Equally important is the issue of cadre management, ensuring that personnel are able to progress through the bureaucratic system in an orderly and productive manner. The issue of deputation continues to be a major cause of concern. Persistent shortages of specialised and efficient staff have raised a debate about a distinct cadre for the IB. It is a paradox that, while the IB is a civil organisation administratively, its functions and practices are purely based on the typical police system. Yet many special benefits given to police personnel, such as departmental accommodation, risk and operational special allowances, vehicles from the rank of sub-inspectors onwards, are denied in the IB. It is neither a police nor a paramilitary organisation, though the IB is treated as one of the Central Police Organisations (CPOs) on many occasions. All these uncertainties and confusions are to be cleared and a transparent system introduced in the IB. It is an unanswerable question as to how police medals are given to IB employees, including supporting/ministerial staff while it is on the list as a civilian organisation.

After the Emergency in 1977, a new government led by the then Janata Party came into power and during this period some directly recruited officers of the IB tried to form an association to vent their grievances as there was no proper forum within the department to hear and redress the genuine problems of the employees. Following instructions from the then government, the IB tried to form a grievance cell for the sake of it, but it never functioned effectively or efficiently. Immediately after the return of the Congress government at the Centre, the IB managed to get the government nod to have three leaders of the association dismissed from service under Article 311(C) on grounds of security. It shows how powerful the IB is.

An important need is to have clarity in the functioning of the IB by definition; legislation should be precise because its words have legal implications. There is reason to believe that IB bosses do not want to bring any legislation to control the functioning of the activities of the IB. The enormous powers provided to intelligence agencies should be carefully spelt out in a legislature format to ensure that they are viewed with all the seriousness they deserve. There should be no room for misinterpreting the authority or task of the agency. A quick look at the US Intelligence Reform and Terrorism Prevention Act of 2004 will reveal precise and detailed wording, spelling out duties, responsibilities and authorities.

In March 2011, Mr. Manish Tiwari, MP, who also subsequently served as a minister in the UPA government, introduced a private member's bill to regulate the manner of functioning and exercise of powers of Indian intelligence agencies. The Bill aimed to regulate the agencies within the country and outside it and aimed at providing for the coordination, control and oversight of such agencies. One of the aims of the bill was to provide legislative authority for the functioning of the agency and the other was to ensure against the misuse of powers. The Bill also provided for a National Intelligence Security Oversight Committee headed by the Chairman of the Rajya Sabha, the Speaker of the Lok Sabha, the Prime Minister, the Home Minister, the Leader of the Opposition in the two houses of Parliament and two MPs nominated by the Chairman of the Rajya Sabha and the Lok Sabha Speaker. The Cabinet Secretary would be the Secretary of the Committee. This Committee would draw up and table an Annual Report, appoint an Intelligence Ombudsman to deal with the staff grievances and administrative issues of the agencies and constitute a National Intelligence Tribunal to investigate complaints against the agencies. Alas, the Bill remains in the long queue of legislation waiting to be put to vote.

On February 24, 2015, the Observer Research Foundation (NGO, New Delhi) published a report that contained the following:

- Improvement is needed in coordination and tasking among intelligence agencies and between state and central agencies.

- Intelligence collection is ad-hoc in the absence of clear-cut requirements from the consumers of intelligence.

- Poor cadre management and the inability to recruit specialists have resulted in shortage of personnel.

- Lack of intellectual capacity and investment in the education system exacerbate recruitment shortfalls in intelligence agencies.

- Agencies suffer from chronic shortage of military expertise and engage private players for specialist tasks. Big data analytics capabilities need to be commissioned and customised for the Indian context.

♦ Special forces capabilities need to be ramped up and their use 'married' with the capabilities of intelligence agencies.

♦ China's growth and the multiplication of its capabilities requires a more focused effort in technical intelligence and human intelligence.

♦ A paramilitary statute is key for creating accountability in intelligence agencies.

♦ Lack of political attention and effective guidance has prevented reformed and optimal functioning of the intelligence system.

The reports of the various committees and commissions, including the Shankaran Nair Commission Report and other subsequent reports that are still kept in the IB archives in its dark room in Delhi, are to be unearthed and brought to light. These recommendations, once disclosed and made available to IB employees, would at least give the employees an opportunity to come to know what is in these reports. There should be political will and, above all, sincere and honest efforts by the IB bosses to implement these recommendations. To sum up, there is an urgent need for comprehensive reform and restructuring of the intelligence apparatus. The initiative must come from not only from the political leadership but from the departmental heads to secure the country's strategic interest in the face of phenomenal and unexpected challenges for which a contented and dedicated workforce is indispensable.

REFERENCES AND SUGGESTED READINGS

Chapter 1:

Spies in the puranas, Varuna: Encyclopaedia of Oriental Philosophy and Religion: Hinduism, Nagendra Kr Singh, A. P. Mishra

Rig Veda versus, Arthashastra, Mahabharat versus: sacred-texts.com

Chapter 2:

The science of Intelligence gathering, Intelligence cycle: fas.org,

Wikipedia, intelligencecareers.gov.

Intelligence gathering cycle is a widely known science, something that is used as an accepted methodology in many fields outside of security studies as well.

Fas.org website of the federation of American scientists is a good place to gather further information on various threat analysis including biological and nuclear weapons, energy related and other defence topics. Intelligence cycle from a security standpoint is well explained and was referred to by the author and would act as a very good future reference for any student of intelligence sciences.

Chapter 3:

List of DIBs, Ranks and Insignia: Wikipedia

Chapter 7:

List of terrorist attacks in India: Wikipedia

Chapter 9:

cdc.gov has an immense amount of information in biological attacks through history as well as potential risks in today's world. Bioterrorism is discussed as well. The author has referred to the material for understanding the topic in detail and has used quotes and examples. The author quotes cdc.gov has a good read for anyone who wants to study the topic of pandemics and the work done by cdc.

Chapter 12:

Case Studies in Information Warfare and Security for Researchers, Teachers and students, Mathew Warren

Chinese entry into power sector raises security fears, Jan 2017, Economic times.

The Political Power of Social Media, By Clay Shirky, Jan 2011, Foreign Affairs Magazine.

Democracy in Cyberspace, Ian Bremmer, Nov 2010, Foreign affairs magazine.

Foreign affairs magazine continues to be one of the most informative when it comes of current affairs and security analysis. The author, who has been in a job that demands being abreast in international affairs topics has been a subscriber for more than a decade. The articles in the magazine usually are from top bureaucrats as well as eminent personalities who have held US defence and political offices. These articles are highly recommended for any student of security analysis and international affairs.

Chapter 13:

Money laundering stages: unodc.org

United Nations Office on Drugs and Crime (UNODC) initiative of the United Nations Organization fights against the evils of illegal narcotic and human trafficking. Their website has ample information on the subject and is a very good reference on the issue of money laundering, which is tied tightly to drugs and human trafficking.

The stages on money laundering is well explained and is available for reference by security agencies all around the world. This book has referred to it as well. Money laundering is usually a borderless crime and fighting it means cooperation between many global agencies and regulators. The UNODC acts as the central control for cooperation, enforcement and sharing of information between nations in this regard.

Financial Action Task Force (FATF), in its role as a global money laundering and terrorist financing watchdog sets international standards to check the spread of these evils. Set up in 1989, the body has been playing a key role in bringing to the forefront the need for the world nations to act together, and how terrorism feeds on laundered money. Its been instrumental in invoking the political will to enact national legislations to combat laundering.

FATF's publications are a great source for study of money laundering and methods to fight it. FATF has engaged with multiple countries including India in understanding the trends and newer methods employed by the launderer in various geographies. FATF then socializes through its publications, the examples that are sent to it by each country. This book refers to the two examples that was sent by India and was published in FATFs publication on 'FATF Oct 2013 Report on Role of hawala and similar in MLTF'.

The book also points to the definition provided by FATF for Hawala and Other Similar Service Provider (HOSSP), as the most accurate definition of the same.

Chapter 20:

Maslow's Hierarchy of Needs article on Simplypsychology. org provides for a great read on human needs, something that was originally published in a 1943 paper titled "A Theory of Human Motivation" by Abraham Maslow . The hierarchy is fundamental to human behavioural studies and acts as guidelines for human resource departments when measuring employees' path to feeling rewarded and fulfilled. Importance to Human assets and their mental and psychological health is found its way into the culture of management of businesses. The importance of these human factors is yet to reach government services, especially security services.